ESSENTIALS

of Supply Chain Management

Michael Hugos

John Wiley & Sons, Inc.

ISBN 0-471-23517-2

Printed in the United States of America.

10 9 8 7 6 5 4

To my wife, Venetia

Contents

Preface

All around us the networking and inter-networking of our economy is taking place. Companies that do business together are linking up electronically. They are doing this to better coordinate their actions and drive costs out of their business operations.

Business in this emerging networked world is as much about process as it is about product. This is because market forces, driven by the speed of communications that electronic networks now make possible, are making product life cycles shorter and shorter. Customer tastes and requirements change quickly. Product inventories are always in danger of becoming obsolete.

To counter this trend, companies are building up their expertise and efficiencies in the process of designing and building new products and in the process of delivering and servicing existing products. Companies that develop higher skill levels in these areas are clearly better able to ride the waves of change and profit from developments in the markets they serve.

The processes involved in the designing, building, and delivering of products to the customers that need them have come to be collectively referred to as supply chain management. No one company can develop high skill levels in all areas of supply chain management so companies are focusing on developing and building their particular strengths, their core competencies. Companies are defining the roles they want to play in the markets they serve and linking up with other companies that have complementary skill sets. This is the dynamic that is driving the formation of modern supply chains.

This book is written especially for two groups of readers. It is written for the senior executive who must decide what kind of supply chain their organization needs and how much to spend to get it. It is also written for the manager who is or soon will be responsible for building and operating some part of his/her company's supply chain. The concepts and techniques presented here serve to create a common frame of reference that both senior executives and line managers can use when communicating with each other about supply chain management issues.

Chapters 1–3 provide an executive overview of the basic principles and the business operations that drive supply chain performance. Chapters 4–5 present techniques, technologies, and metrics to use in coordinating your operations with those of your supply chain partners. In Chapters 6 and 7 there is a pragmatic approach to use for defining supply chain opportunities and for designing and building the systems needed to effectively respond to those opportunities. The last chapter, Chapter 8, outlines the profit potential now available to companies that learn to harness the power of the real-time supply chain.

Acknowledgments

I n numerous places in this book you will see mention made of a company named Network Services Company or "Network" for short. Network (http://www.nsconline.com) is a national cooperative of distribution companies who service national and local customers all over North America. I am Network's Chief Information Officer and have had the opportunity these last several years to help the company design, build, and deploy a suite of supply chain management and e-business systems. These systems help us ride the wave of business developments now shaping the markets we serve. We take an utterly pragmatic approach to this undertaking. We have succeeded more often than not and have learned much along the way.

I would like to thank the Network member companies who are also the owners of the organization. Without their backing and active participation there would be no success. I would like to thank the management and staff of Network itself. They have built an outstanding company that I am privileged to be a part of. I wish to give special thanks to the managers and staff of the Information Technology groups of Network and its member companies. They have done amazing things.

I am indebted (more than I even know) to my wife Venetia. She patiently supported me while I wrote this book. She became a weekend widow as I secluded myself in my study to write these pages. She read chapters, kept me from going off on tangents, and provided sound advice.

I want to thank my friend Percy for all his input and assistance. Also thank you to my friend Kelly David—his recent CD often provided the music I needed to find the way through to the end of this book.

CHAPTER 1

Basic Concepts of Supply Chain Management

After reading this chapter you will be able to

- Appreciate what a supply chain is and what it does
- Define the different organizations that participate in any supply chain
- Discuss ways to align your supply chain with your business strategy
- Start an intelligent conversation about the supply chain management issues in your company

Supply chains encompass the companies and the business activities needed to design, make, deliver, and use a product or service. Businesses depend on their supply chains to provide them with what they need to survive and thrive. Every business fits into one or more supply chains and has a role to play in each of them.

The pace of change and the uncertainty about how markets will evolve has made it increasingly important for companies to be aware of the supply chains they participate in and to understand the roles that they play. Those companies that learn how to build and participate in strong supply chains will have a substantial competitive advantage in their markets.

1

Nothing Entirely New...Just a Significant Evolution

The practice of supply chain management is guided by some basic underlying concepts that have not changed much over the centuries. Several hundred years ago, Napoleon made the remark, "An army marches on its stomach." Napoleon was a master strategist and a skillful general and this remark shows that he clearly understood the importance of what we would now call an efficient supply chain. Unless the soldiers are fed, the army cannot move.

Along these same lines, there is another saying that goes, "Amateurs talk strategy and professionals talk logistics." People can discuss all sorts of grand strategies and dashing maneuvers but none of that will be possible without first figuring out how to meet the day-to-day demands of providing an army with fuel, spare parts, food, shelter, and ammunition. It is the seemingly mundane activities of the quartermaster and the supply sergeants that often determine an army's success. This has many analogies in business.

The term "supply chain management" arose in the late 1980s and came into widespread use in the 1990s. Prior to that time, businesses used terms such as "logistics" and "operations management" instead. Some definitions of a supply chain are offered below:

- "A supply chain is the alignment of firms that bring products or services to market."—from Lambert, Stock, and Ellram in their book *Fundamentals of Logistics Management* (Lambert, Douglas M., James R. Stock, and Lisa M. Ellram, 1998, *Fundamentals of Logistics Management*, Boston, MA: Irwin/McGraw-Hill, Chapter 14)

- "A supply chain consists of all stages involved, directly or indirectly, in fulfilling a customer request. The supply chain not only includes the manufacturer and suppliers, but also transporters, warehouses, retailers, and customers themselves."—from Chopra and Meindl in their book *Supply*

Chain Management: Strategy, Planning, and Operations (Chopra, Sunil, and Peter Meindl, 2001, *Supply Chain Management: Strategy, Planning, and Operations*, Upper Saddle River, NJ: Prentice-Hall, Inc. Chapter 1).

- "A supply chain is a network of facilities and distribution options that performs the functions of procurement of materials, transformation of these materials into intermediate and finished products, and the distribution of these finished products to customers."—from Ganeshan and Harrison at Penn State University in their article *An Introduction to Supply Chain Management* published at http://silmaril.smeal.psu.edu/supply_chain_intro.html (Ganeshan, Ram, and Terry P. Harrison, 1995, "An Introduction to Supply Chain Management," Department of Management Sciences and Information Systems, 303 Beam Business Building, Penn State University, University Park, PA).

If this is what a supply chain is then we can define supply chain management as the things we do to influence the behavior of the supply chain and get the results we want. Some definitions of supply chain management are:

- "The systemic, strategic coordination of the traditional business functions and the tactics across these business functions within a particular company and across businesses within the supply chain, for the purposes of improving the long-term performance of the individual companies and the supply chain as a whole."—from Mentzer, DeWitt, Deebler, Min, Nix, Smith, and Zacharia in their article *Defining Supply Chain Management* in the *Journal of Business Logistics* (Mentzer, John T., William DeWitt, James S. Keebler, Soonhong Min, Nancy W. Nix, Carlo D. Smith, and Zach G. Zacharia, 2001, "Defining Supply Chain Management," *Journal of Business Logistics*, Vol. 22, No. 2, p. 18).

- "Supply chain management is the coordination of production, inventory, location, and transportation among the participants in a supply chain to achieve the best mix of responsiveness and efficiency for the market being served."—my own words.

There is a difference between the concept of supply chain management and the traditional concept of logistics. Logistics typically refers to activities that occur within the boundaries of a single organization and supply chains refer to networks of companies that work together and coordinate their actions to deliver a product to market. Also traditional logistics focuses its attention on activities such as procurement, distribution, maintenance, and inventory management. Supply chain management acknowledges all of traditional logistics and also includes activities such as marketing, new product development, finance, and customer service.

In the wider view of supply chain thinking, these additional activities are now seen as part of the work needed to fulfill customer requests. Supply chain management views the supply chain and the organizations in it as a single entity. It brings a systems approach to understanding and managing the different activities needed to coordinate the flow of products and services to best serve the ultimate customer. This systems approach provides the framework in which to best respond to business requirements that otherwise would seem to be in conflict with each other.

Taken individually, different supply chain requirements often have conflicting needs. For instance, the requirement of maintaining high levels of customer service calls for maintaining high levels of inventory, but then the requirement to operate efficiently calls for reducing inventory levels. It is only when these requirements are seen together as parts of a larger picture that ways can be found to effectively balance their different demands.

Effective supply chain management requires simultaneous improvements in both customer service levels and the internal operating efficiencies of the companies in the supply chain. Customer service at its most basic level means consistently high order fill rates, high on-time delivery rates, and a very low rate of products returned by customers for whatever reason. Internal efficiency for organizations in a supply chain means that these organizations get an attractive rate of return on their investments in inventory and other assets and that they find ways to lower their operating and sales expenses.

There is a basic pattern to the practice of supply chain management. Each supply chain has its own unique set of market demands and operating challenges and yet the issues remain essentially the same in every case. Companies in any supply chain must make decisions individually and collectively regarding their actions in five areas:

1. *Production*—What products does the market want? How much of which products should be produced and by when? This activity includes the creation of master production schedules that take into account plant capacities, workload balancing, quality control, and equipment maintenance.

2. *Inventory*—What inventory should be stocked at each stage in a supply chain? How much inventory should be held as raw materials, semifinished, or finished goods? The primary purpose of inventory is to act as a buffer against uncertainty in the supply chain. However, holding inventory can be expensive, so what are the optimal inventory levels and reorder points?

3. *Location*—Where should facilities for production and inventory storage be located? Where are the most cost efficient locations for production and for storage of inventory? Should existing facilities be used or new ones built? Once these decisions are made they determine the possible paths available for product to flow through for delivery to the final consumer.

4. *Transportation*—How should inventory be moved from one supply chain location to another? Air freight and truck delivery are generally fast and reliable but they are expensive. Shipping by sea or rail is much less expensive but usually involves longer transit times and more uncertainty. This uncertainty must be compensated for by stocking higher levels of inventory. When is it better to use which mode of transportation?

5. *Information*—How much data should be collected and how much information should be shared? Timely and accurate information holds the promise of better coordination and better decision making. With good information, people can make effective decisions about what to produce and how much, about where to locate inventory and how best to transport it.

The sum of these decisions will define the capabilities and effectiveness of a company's supply chain. The things a company can do and the ways that it can compete in its markets are all very much dependent on the effectiveness of its supply chain. If a company's strategy is to serve a mass market and compete on the basis of price, it had better have a supply chain that is optimized for low cost. If a company's strategy is to serve a market segment and compete on the basis of customer service and convenience, it had better have a supply chain optimized for responsiveness. Who a company is and what it can do is shaped by its supply chain and by the markets it serves.

How the Supply Chain Works

Two influential source books that define principles and practice of supply chain management are *The Goal* (Goldratt, Eliyahu M., 1984, *The Goal*, Great Barrington, MA: The North River Press Publishing Corporation); and *Supply Chain Management: Strategy, Planning, and Operation* by Sunil Chopra and Peter Meindl. *The Goal* explores the

IN THE REAL WORLD

Alexander the Great based his strategies and campaigns on his army's unique capabilities and these were made possible by effective supply chain management.

In the spirit of the saying, "amateurs talk strategy and professionals talk logistics," let's look at the campaigns of Alexander the Great. For those who think that his greatness was only due to his ability to dream up bold moves and cut a dashing figure in the saddle, think again. Alexander was a master of supply chain management and he could not have succeeded otherwise. The authors from Greek and Roman times who recorded his deeds had little to say about something so apparently unglamourous as how he secured supplies for his army. Yet, from these same sources, many little details can be pieced together to show the overall supply chain picture and how Alexander managed it. A modern historian, Donald Engels, has investigated this topic in his book *Alexander the Great and the Logistics of the Macedonian Army* (Engles, Donald W., 1978, *Alexander the Great and the Logistics of the Macedonian Army*, Los Angeles, CA: University of California Press).

He begins by pointing out that given the conditions and the technology that existed in Alexander's time, his strategy and tactics had to be very closely tied to his ability to get supplies and to run a lean, efficient organization. The only way to transport large amounts of material over long distances was by ocean-going ships or by barges on rivers and canals. Once away from rivers and sea coasts, an army had to be able to live off the land over which it traveled. Diminishing returns set in quickly when using pack animals and carts to haul supplies because the animals themselves had to eat and would soon consume all the food and water they were hauling unless they could graze along the way.

Alexander's army was able to achieve its brilliant successes because it managed its supply chain so well. The army had a logistics structure that was fundamentally different from other armies of the time. In other armies the number of support people and camp followers was often as large as the number of actual fighting soldiers because armies traveled with huge numbers of carts and pack animals to carry their equipment and provisions, as well as the people needed to tend them. In the Macedonian army the use of carts was severly restricted. Soldiers were trained to carry their own equipment and provisions. Other contemporary armies did not require their soldiers to carry such heavy burdens but they paid for this because the resulting baggage trains reduced their speed and mobility.

The result of the Macedonian army's logistics structure was that it became the fastest, lightest, and most mobile army of its time. It was capable of making lightning strikes against an opponent often before they were even aware of what was happening. Because the army was able to move quickly and suddenly, Alexander could use this capability to devise strategies and employ tactics that allowed him to surprise and overwhelm enemies that were numerically much larger.

The picture that emerges of how Alexander managed his supply chain is an interesting one. For instance, time and again the historical sources mention that before he entered a new territory, he would receive the surrender of its ruler and arrange in advance with local officials for the supplies his army would need. If a region did not surrender to him in advance, Alexander would not commit his entire army to a campaign in that land. He would not risk putting his army in a situation where it could be crippled or destroyed by a lack of provisions. Instead, he would gather intelligence about the routes, the resources, and the climate of the region and then set off with a small, light force to surprise his opponent. The main army would remain behind at a well-stocked base until Alexander secured adequate supplies for it to follow.

Whenever the army set up a new base it looked for an area that provided easy access to a navigable river or a seaport. Then ships would arrive from other parts of Alexander's empire bringing in large amounts of supplies. The army always stayed in its winter camp until the first spring harvest of the new year so that food supplies would be available. When it marched, it avoided dry or uninhabited areas and moved through river valleys and populated regions whenever possible so the horses could graze and the army could requisition supplies along the route.

Alexander had a deep understanding of the capabilities and limitations of his supply chain. He learned well how to formulate strategies and use tactics that built upon the unique strengths that his logistics and supply chain capabilities gave him and he wisely took measures to compensate for the limitations of his supply chain. His opponents often outnumbered him and were usually fighting on their own home territory. Yet their advantages were undermined by clumsy and inefficient supply chains that restricted their ability to act and limited their options for opposing Alexander's moves.

issues and provides answers to the problem of optimizing operations in any business system whether it be manufacturing, mortgage loan processing, or supply chain management. *Supply Chain Management: Strategy, Planning, and Operation* is an in-depth presentation of the concepts and techniques of the profession. Much of the material presented in this chapter and in the next two chapters can be found in greater detail in these two books.

The goal or mission of supply chain management can be defined using Mr. Goldratt's words as "Increase throughput while simultaneously reducing both inventory and operating expense." In this definition throughput refers to the rate at which sales to the end customer occur. Depending on the market being served, sales or throughput occurs for different reasons. In some markets customers value and will pay for high levels of service. In other markets customers seek simply the lowest price for an item.

As we saw in the previous section, there are five areas where companies can make decisions that will define their supply chain capabilities: Production; Inventory; Location; Transportation; and Information. Chopra and Meindl define these areas as performance drivers that can be managed to produce the capabilities needed for a given supply chain.

Effective supply chain management calls first for an understanding of each driver and how it operates. Each driver has the ability to directly affect the supply chain and enable certain capabilities. The next step is to develop an appreciation for the results that can be obtained by mixing different combinations of these drivers. Let's start by looking at the drivers individually.

Production

Production refers to the capacity of a supply chain to make and store products. The facilities of production are factories and warehouses. The fundamental decision that managers face when making production decisions is how to resolve the trade-off between responsiveness and efficiency. If factories and warehouses are built with a lot of excess capacity, they can be very flexible and respond quickly to wide swings in product demand. Facilities where all or almost all capacity is being used are not capable of responding easily to fluctuations in demand. On the other hand, capacity costs money and excess capacity is idle capacity not in use and not generating revenue. So the more excess capacity that exists, the less efficient the operation becomes.

Factories can be built to accommodate one of two approaches to manufacturing:

1. *Product focus*—A factory that takes a product focus performs the range of different operations required to make a given product

line from fabrication of different product parts to assembly of these parts.

2. *Functional focus*—A functional approach concentrates on performing just a few operations such as only making a select group of parts or only doing assembly. These functions can be applied to making many different kinds of products.

A product approach tends to result in developing expertise about a given set of products at the expense of expertise about any particular function. A functional approach results in expertise about particular functions instead of expertise in a given product. Companies need to decide which approach or what mix of these two approaches will give them the capability and expertise they need to best respond to customer demands.

As with factories, warehouses too can be built to accommodate different approaches. There are three main approaches to use in warehousing:

1. *Stock keeping unit (SKU) storage*—In this traditional approach, all of a given type of product is stored together. This is an efficient and easy to understand way to store products.

2. *Job lot storage*—In this approach, all the different products related to the needs of a certain type of customer or related to the needs of a particular job are stored together. This allows for an efficient picking and packing operation but usually requires more storage space than the traditional SKU storage approach.

3. *Crossdocking*—An approach that was pioneered by Wal-Mart in its drive to increase efficiencies in its supply chain. In this approach, product is not actually warehoused in the facility. Instead the facility is used to house a process where trucks from suppliers arrive and unload large quantities of different products. These large lots are then broken down into smaller lots. Smaller lots of different products are recombined according to the needs of the day and quickly loaded onto outbound trucks that deliver the products to their final destination.

Inventory

Inventory is spread throughout the supply chain and includes everything from raw material to work in process to finished goods that are held by the manufacturers, distributors, and retailers in a supply chain. Again, managers must decide where they want to position themselves in the trade-off between responsiveness and efficiency. Holding large amounts of inventory allows a company or an entire supply chain to be very responsive to fluctuations in customer demand. However, the creation and storage of inventory is a cost and to achieve high levels of efficiency, the cost of inventory should be kept as low as possible.

There are three basic decisions to make regarding the creation and holding of inventory:

1. *Cycle Inventory*—This is the amount of inventory needed to satisfy demand for the product in the period between purchases of the product. Companies tend to produce and to purchase in large lots in order to gain the advantages that economies of scale can bring. However, with large lots also comes increased carrying costs. Carrying costs come from the cost to store, handle, and insure the inventory. Managers face the trade-off between the reduced cost of ordering and better prices offered by purchasing product in large lots and the increased carrying cost of the cycle inventory that comes with purchasing in large lots.

2. *Safety Inventory*—Inventory that is held as a buffer against uncertainty. If demand forecasting could be done with perfect accuracy,

then the only inventory that would be needed would be cycle inventory. But since every forecast has some degree of uncertainty in it, we cover that uncertainty to a greater or lesser degree by holding additional inventory in case demand is suddenly greater than anticipated. The trade-off here is to weigh the costs of carrying extra inventory against the costs of losing sales due to insufficient inventory.

3. *Seasonal Inventory*—This is inventory that is built up in anticipation of predictable increases in demand that occur at certain times of the year. For example, it is predictable that demand for anti-freeze will increase in the winter. If a company that makes anti-freeze has a fixed production rate that is expensive to change, then it will try to manufacture product at a steady rate all year long and build up inventory during periods of low demand to cover for periods of high demand that will exceed its production rate. The alternative to building up seasonal inventory is to invest in flexible manufacturing facilities that can quickly change their rate of production of different products to respond to increases in demand. In this case, the trade-off is between the cost of carrying seasonal inventory and the cost of having more flexible production capabilities.

Location

Location refers to the geographical siting of supply chain facilities. It also includes the decisions related to which activities should be performed in each facility. The responsiveness versus efficiency trade-off here is the decision whether to centralize activities in fewer locations to gain economies of scale and efficiency, or to decentralize activities in many locations close to customers and suppliers in order for operations to be more responsive.

When making location decisions, managers need to consider a range of factors that relate to a given location including the cost of facilities, the cost of labor, skills available in the workforce, infrastructure conditions, taxes and tariffs, and proximity to suppliers and customers. Location decisions tend to be very strategic decisions because they commit large amounts of money to long-term plans.

Location decisions have strong impacts on the cost and performance characteristics of a supply chain. Once the size, number, and location of facilities is determined, that also defines the number of possible paths through which products can flow on the way to the final customer. Location decisions reflect a company's basic strategy for building and delivering its products to market.

Transportation

This refers to the movement of everything from raw material to finished goods between different facilities in a supply chain. In transportation the trade-off between responsiveness and efficiency is manifested in the choice of transport mode. Fast modes of transport such as airplanes are very responsive but also more costly. Slower modes such as ship and rail are very cost efficient but not as responsive. Since transportation costs can be as much as a third of the operating cost of a supply chain, decisions made here are very important.

There are six basic modes of transport that a company can choose from:

1. *Ship* which is very cost efficient but also the slowest mode of transport. It is limited to use between locations that are situated next to navigable waterways and facilities such as harbors and canals.

2. *Rail* which is also very cost efficient but can be slow. This mode is also restricted to use between locations that are served by rail lines.

14

3. *Pipelines* can be very efficient but are restricted to commodities that are liquids or gases such as water, oil, and natural gas.

4. *Trucks* are a relatively quick and very flexible mode of transport. Trucks can go almost anywhere. The cost of this mode is prone to fluctuations though, as the cost of fuel fluctuates and the condition of roads varies.

5. *Airplanes* are a very fast mode of transport and are very responsive. This is also the most expensive mode and it is somewhat limited by the availability of appropriate airport facilities.

6. *Electronic Transport* is the fastest mode of transport and it is very flexible and cost efficient. However, it can only be used for movement of certain types of products such as electric energy, data, and products composed of data such as music, pictures, and text. Someday technology that allows us to convert matter to energy and back to matter again may completely rewrite the theory and practice of supply chain management ("beam me up, Scotty...").

Given these different modes of transportation and the location of the facilities in a supply chain, managers need to design routes and networks for moving products. A route is the path through which products move and networks are composed of the collection of the paths and facilities connected by those paths. As a general rule, the higher the value of a product (such as electronic components or pharmaceuticals), the more its transport network should emphasize responsiveness and the lower the value of a product (such as bulk commodities like grain or lumber), the more its network should emphasize efficiency.

Information

Information is the basis upon which to make decisions regarding the other four supply chain drivers. It is the connection between all of the activities and operations in a supply chain. To the extent that this connection is a strong one, (i.e., the data is accurate, timely, and complete), the companies in a supply chain will each be able to make good decisions for their own operations. This will also tend to maximize the profitability of the supply chain as a whole. That is the way that stock markets or other free markets work and supply chains have many of the same dynamics as markets.

Information is used for two purposes in any supply chain:

1. *Coordinating daily activities* related to the functioning of the other four supply chain drivers: production; inventory; location; and transportation. The companies in a supply chain use available data on product supply and demand to decide on weekly production schedules, inventory levels, transportation routes, and stocking locations.

2. *Forecasting and planning* to anticipate and meet future demands. Available information is used to make tactical forecasts to guide the setting of monthly and quarterly production schedules and timetables. Information is also used for strategic forecasts to guide decisions about whether to build new facilities, enter a new market, or exit an existing market.

Within an individual company the trade-off between responsiveness and efficiency involves weighing the benefits that good information can provide against the cost of acquiring that information. Abundant, accurate information can enable very efficient operating decisions and better forecasts but the cost of building and installing systems to deliver this information can be very high.

Within the supply chain as a whole, the responsiveness versus efficiency trade-off that companies make is one of deciding how much information to share with the other companies and how much information

TIPS & TECHNIQUES

The Five Major
Supply Chain Drivers

1. **PRODUCTION** What, how, and when to produce	**2.** **INVENTORY** How much to make and how much to store
5. **INFORMATION** The basis for making these decisions	
4. **TRANSPORTATION** How and when to move product	**3.** **LOCATION** Where best to do what activity

RESPONSIVENESS versus EFFICIENCY

The right combination of responsiveness and efficiency in each of these drivers allows a supply chain to "increase throughput while simultaneously reducing inventory and operating expense."

Each market or group of customers has a specific set of needs. The supply chains that serve different markets need to respond effectively to these needs. Some markets demand and will pay for high levels of responsiveness. Other markets require their supply chains to focus more on efficiency. The overall effect of the decisions made concerning each driver will determine how well the supply chain serves its market and how profitable it is for the participants in that supply chain.

to keep private. The more information about product supply, customer demand, market forecasts, and production schedules that companies share with each other, the more responsive everyone can be. Balancing this openness however, are the concerns that each company has about revealing information that could be used against it by a competitor. The potential costs associated with increased competition can hurt the profitability of a company.

EXECUTIVE INSIGHT

Wal-Mart is a company shaped by its supply chain and the efficiency of its supply chain has made it a leader in the markets it serves.

Sam Walton decided to build a company that would serve a mass market and compete on the basis of price. He did this by creating one of the world's most efficient supply chains. The structure and operations of this company have been defined by the need to lower its costs and increase its productivity so that it could pass these savings on to its customers in the form of lower prices. The techniques that Wal-Mart pioneered are now being widely adopted by its competitors and by other companies serving entirely different markets.

Wal-Mart introduced concepts that are now industry standards. Many of these concepts come directly from the way the company builds and operates its supply chain. Let's look at four such concepts:

❶ The strategy of expanding around distribution centers (DCs)

❷ Using electronic data interchange (EDI) with suppliers

❸ The "big box" store format

❹ "Everyday low prices"

The strategy of expanding around DCs is central to the way Wal-Mart enters a new geographical market. The company looks for areas that can support a group of new stores, not just a single new store. It then builds a new DC at a central location in the area and opens its first store at the same time. The DC is the supply chain bridgehead into the new territory. It supports the opening of more new stores in the area at a very low additional cost. Those savings are passed along to the customers.

The use of EDI with suppliers provides the company two substantial benefits. First of all this cuts the transaction costs associated with the ordering of products and the paying of invoices. Ordering products and paying invoices are, for the most part, well defined and routine processes that can be made very productive and efficient through EDI. The second benefit is that these electronic links with suppliers allow Wal-Mart a high degree of control and coordination in the scheduling and receiving of product deliveries. This helps to ensure a steady flow of the right products at the right time, delivered to the right DCs, by all Wal-Mart suppliers.

The big box store format allows Wal-Mart to, in effect, combine a store and a warehouse in a single facility and get great operating efficiencies from doing so. The big box is big enough to hold large amounts of inventory like a warehouse. And since this inventory is being held at the same location where the customer buys it, there is no delay or cost that would otherwise be associated with moving products from warehouse to store. Again, these savings are passed along to the customer.

Everyday low prices are a way of doing two things. The first thing is to tell its price-conscious customers that they will always get the best price. They need not look elsewhere or wait for special sales. The effect of this message to customers helps Wal-Mart do the second thing, which is to accurately forecast product sales. By eliminating special sales and assuring customers of low prices, it smoothes out demand swings making demand more steady and predictable. This way stores are more likely to have what customers want when they want it.

Taken individually, these four concepts are each useful but their real power comes from being used in connection with each other. They combine to form a supply chain that drives a self-reinforcing business process. Each concept builds on the strengths of the others to create a powerful business model for a company that has grown to become a dominant player in its markets.

There seem to be some similarities between Wal-Mart and Alexander the Great.

The Evolving Structure of Supply Chains

The participants in a supply chain are continuously making decisions that affect how they manage the five supply chain drivers. Each organization tries to maximize its performance in dealing with these drivers through a combination of outsourcing, partnering, and in-house expertise. In the fast-moving markets of our present economy a company usually will focus on what it considers to be its core competencies in supply chain management and outsource the rest.

This was not always the case though. In the slower moving mass markets of the industrial age it was common for successful companies to attempt to own much of their supply chain. That was known as vertical integration. The aim of vertical integration was to gain maximum efficiency through economies of scale (see Exhibit 1.1).

In the first half of the 1900s Ford Motor Company owned much of what it needed to feed its car factories. It owned and operated iron

EXHIBIT 1.1

Old Supply Chains versus New

Vertically integrated companies serving slow-moving mass markets once attempted to own much of their supply chains. Today's fast-moving markets require more flexible and responsive supply chains.

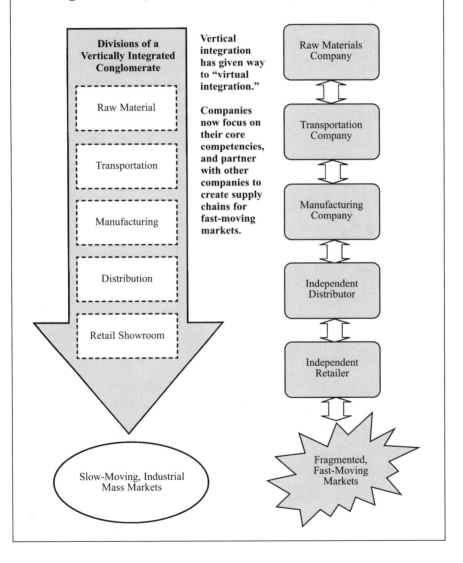

mines that extracted iron ore, steel mills that turned the ore into steel products, plants that made component car parts, and assembly plants that turned out finished cars. In addition, they owned farms where they grew flax to make into linen car tops and forests that they logged and sawmills where they cut the timber into lumber for making wooden car parts. Ford's famous River Rouge Plant was a monument to vertical integration—iron ore went in at one end and cars came out at the other end. Henry Ford in his 1926 autobiography, *Today and Tomorrow*, boasted that his company could take in iron ore from the mine and put out a car 81 hours later (Ford, Henry, 1926, *Today and Tomorrow*, Portland, OR: Productivity Press, Inc.).

This was a profitable way of doing business in the more predictable, one-size-fits-all industrial economy that existed in the early 1900s. Ford and other businesses churned out mass amounts of basic products. But as the markets grew and customers became more particular about the kind of products they wanted, this model began to break down. It could not be responsive enough or produce the variety of products that were being demanded. For instance, when Henry Ford was asked about the number of different colors a customer could request, he said, "they can have any color they want as long as it's black." In the 1920s Ford's market share was over 50 percent but by the 1940s it had fallen to below 20 percent. Focusing on efficiency at the expense of being responsive to customer desires was no longer a successful business model.

Globalization, highly competitive markets, and the rapid pace of technological change are now driving the development of supply chains where multiple companies work together, each company focusing on the activities that it does best. Mining companies focus on mining, timber companies focus on logging and making lumber, and manufacturing companies focus on different types of manufacturing from making component parts to doing final assembly. This way people in each company can keep up with rapid rates of change and keep learning the new skills needed to compete in their particular business.

Where companies once routinely ran their own warehouses or operated their own fleet of trucks, they now have to consider whether those operations are really a core competency or whether it is more cost effective to outsource those operations to other companies that make logistics the center of their business. To achieve high levels of operating efficiency and to keep up with continuing changes in technology, companies need to focus on their core competencies. It requires this kind of focus to stay competitive.

Instead of vertical integration, companies now practice "virtual integration." Companies find other companies who they can work with to perform the activities called for in their supply chains. How a company defines its core competencies and how it positions itself in the supply chains it serves is one of the most important decisions it can make.

Participants in the Supply Chain

In its simplest form, a supply chain is composed of a company and the suppliers and customers of that company. This is the basic group of participants that creates a simple supply chain. Extended supply chains contain three additional types of participants. First there is the supplier's supplier or the ultimate supplier at the beginning of an extended supply chain. Then there is the customer's customer or ultimate customer at the end of an extended supply chain. Finally there is a whole category of companies who are service providers to other companies in the supply chain. These are companies who supply services in logistics, finance, marketing, and information technology.

In any given supply chain there is some combination of companies who perform different functions. There are companies that are producers, distributors or wholesalers, retailers, and companies or individuals who are the customers, the final consumers of a product. Supporting these companies there will be other companies that are service providers that provide a range of needed services.

Producers

Producers or manufacturers are organizations that make a product. This includes companies that are producers of raw materials and companies that are producers of finished goods. Producers of raw materials are organizations that mine for minerals, drill for oil and gas, and cut timber. It also includes organizations that farm the land, raise animals, or catch seafood. Producers of finished goods use the raw materials and sub-assemblies made by other producers to create their products.

Producers can create products that are intangible items such as music, entertainment, software, or designs. A product can also be a service such as mowing a lawn, cleaning an office, performing surgery, or teaching a skill. In many instances the producers of tangible, industrial products are moving to areas of the world where labor is less costly. Producers in the developed world of North America, Europe, and parts of Asia are increasingly producers of intangible items and services.

Distributors

Distributors are companies that take inventory in bulk from producers and deliver a bundle of related product lines to customers. Distributors are also known as wholesalers. They typically sell to other businesses and they sell products in larger quantities than an individual consumer would usually buy. Distributors buffer the producers from fluctuations in product demand by stocking inventory and doing much of the sales work to find and service customers. For the customer, distributors fulfill the "Time and Place" function—they deliver products when and where the customer wants them.

A distributor is typically an organization that takes ownership of significant inventories of products that they buy from producers and sell to consumers. In addition to product promotion and sales, other functions the distributor performs are inventory management, warehouse operations, and product transportation as well as customer support and post-sales service. A distributor can also be an organization that only brokers a product between the producer and the customer and never takes ownership of that product. This kind of distributor performs mainly the functions of product promotion and sales. In both these cases, as the needs of customers evolve and the range of available products changes, the distributor is the agent that continually tracks customer needs and matches them with products available.

Retailers

Retailers stock inventory and sell in smaller quantities to the general public. This organization also closely tracks the preferences and demands of the customers that it sells to. It advertises to its customers and often uses some combination of price, product selection, service, and convenience as the primary draw to attract customers for the products it sells. Discount department stores attract customers using price and wide product selection. Upscale specialty stores offer a unique line of products and high levels of service. Fast food restaurants use convenience and low prices as their draw.

Customers

Customers or consumers are any organization that purchases and uses a product. A customer organization may purchase a product in order to incorporate it into another product that they in turn sell to other customers. Or a customer may be the final end user of a product who buys the product in order to consume it.

Service Providers

These are organizations that provide services to producers, distributors, retailers, and customers. Service providers have developed special expertise and skills that focus on a particular activity needed by a supply chain. Because of this, they are able to perform these services more effectively and at a better price than producers, distributors, retailers, or consumers could do on their own.

Some common service providers in any supply chain are providers of transportation services and warehousing services. These are trucking companies and public warehouse companies and they are known as logistics providers. Financial service providers deliver services such as making loans, doing credit analysis, and collecting on past due invoices. These are banks, credit rating companies, and collection agencies. Some service providers deliver market research and advertising, while others provide product design, engineering services, legal services, and management advice. Still other service providers offer information technology and data collection services. All these service providers are integrated to a greater or lesser degree into the ongoing operations of the producers, distributors, retailers, and consumers in the supply chain.

Supply chains are composed of repeating sets of participants that fall into one or more of these categories. Over time the needs of the supply chain as a whole remain fairly stable. What changes is the mix of participants in the supply chain and the roles that each participant plays. In some supply chains, there are few service providers because the other participants perform these services on their own. In other supply chains very efficient providers of specialized services have evolved and the other participants outsource work to these service providers instead of doing it themselves. Examples of supply chain structure are shown in Exhibit 1.2.

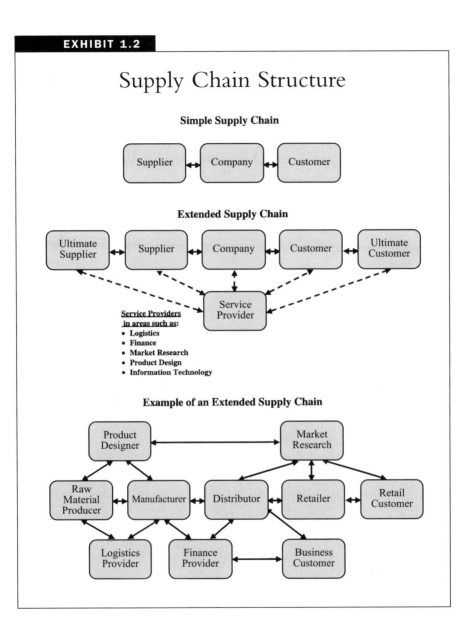

IN THE REAL WORLD

A new category of supply chain service providers has arisen because of opportunities opened up by the use of information technology. Functions that companies each used to do on their own can now be outsourced to companies who make that function a core competency.

SiteStuff (www.sitestuff.com) is a procurement solutions provider focused on the real estate management market. The company serves customers such as Trammell Crow, Jones Lang LaSalle, C.B. Richard Ellis, and Insignia/ESG. Charlie Pace is SiteStuff's chief operating officer and has been with the company since its founding in 1999. Charlie's areas of responsibilities include creating SiteStuff's product offering for maintenance, repair, and operations (MRO) Services and future lines of business, supply chain operations, and relationships with suppliers.

"Our founder, Michael Stuart, was a CIO for several REITS (real estate investment trusts). Back in the 1980s he saw the need in the property management industry for better budgeting support based on more detailed understanding of spending patterns," said Charlie. "He put together a plan to offer this solution to property managers before the Internet, but it was too expensive. Then the Internet came along and suddenly it became possible to cheaply network into thousands of commercial properties."

Traditionally, real estate procurement has been very decentralized and real estate companies have shared similar issues when purchasing maintenance, repair, and operations (MRO) products and services. This decentralized purchasing process results in:

- A lack of compliance on national purchasing contracts
- High transaction costs due to working with thousands of vendors
- Lack of visibility into property operations

IN THE REAL WORLD (CONTINUED)

"SiteStuff helps owners and managers of real estate save money, save time, and gain control over property operations by aggregating their buying power, streamlining back-end accounting practices, and allowing them to more effectively track and manage data regarding procurement activities," Charlie explained. "I think most people can see the benefits conceptually. The hard part is to do it in practice. In our daily operations we focus on three areas to get the job done.

"The first and most difficult is change management. We are fundamentally changing the way distribution works with the properties and vice versa. We put together national solutions for what up until now have been regional markets. Distributors now have to deliver a very specific and predefined set of products.

"Technology infrastructure is the second area. Managing the order fulfillment process, which includes collecting end user data, order status, etc., is one of our core activities. This calls for us to roll out an e-purchasing system to our customers as well as link our supplier's systems with internal tools in order to provide seamless integration.

"Changing perceptions so that SiteStuff becomes an accepted channel to market—that's the third. We have successfully demonstrated to property managers, manufacturers, and distributors that our procurement solution delivers quantifiable benefits to all parties. Initially, this was a difficult proposition to prove, however, we gained traction as our volume quickly ramped up."

SiteStuff did a strategic sourcing assessment for its customers based on 1999 purchasing data provided by the customers. The study identified the MRO products and services that customers were buying, what the brand preferences were, whose products performed the best, and who had the best pricing. With this data, SiteStuff could zero in on the best-in-class providers of products and services for its customers. They then began a process of negotiating national contracts with these providers.

"For manufacturers we offer them the ability to drive standardization with our customers. Through distributor rationalization, we partner with a few best-in-class distributors per category, which in turn offers them a significant increase in the business they get from our properties. And our customers now have access to a single-source, paperless process for purchasing all of their MRO products. They outsource their purchasing operations and benefit from better economies of scale. For each constituent in our model, we provide high levels of data on purchasing activities, customer profiles, and seasonal patterns. We are bringing transparency to the supply chain."

In reflecting on the last couple of years, Charlie summarized the main lessons learned. "We have to stay very focused on our core proposition. We do purchasing of MRO products and services for people who manage real estate. We continue to build our value in that area. We have learned how best to roll out the technology and how to integrate with our supplier partners. We also have learned a lot about how to screen suppliers for their ability to implement our technology and how to support and assist our client to grow with us."

Looking at the next couple of years, Charlie sees the company continuing to grow its client base. "We know we have an excellent procurement solution in place now. We will continue to grow and enhance our facility management service offerings. We will further integrate our systems with those of suppliers. Where there is real estate and a need to manage it, we have a solution and real estate leaders are starting to realize that."

Aligning the Supply Chain with Business Strategy

A company's supply chain is an integral part of its approach to the markets it serves. The supply chain needs to respond to market requirements and do so in a way that supports the company's business strategy. The business strategy a company employs starts with the needs of the customers that the company serves or will serve. Depending on the needs of its customers, a company's supply chain must deliver the appropriate mix of responsiveness and efficiency. A company whose supply chain allows it to more efficiently meet the needs of its customers will gain market share at the expense of other companies in that market and also will be more profitable.

For example, let's consider two companies and the needs that their supply chains must respond to. The two companies are 7-Eleven and Sam's Club, which is a part of Wal-Mart. The customers who shop at convenience stores like 7-Eleven have a different set of needs and preferences from those who shop at a discount warehouse like Sam's Club. The 7-Eleven customer is looking for convenience and not the lowest price. That customer is often in a hurry and prefers that the store be close by and have enough variety of products so that they can pick up small amounts of common household or food items that they need immediately. Sam's Club customers are looking for the lowest price. They are not in a hurry and are willing to drive some distance and buy large quantities of limited numbers of items in order to get the lowest price possible.

Clearly the supply chain for 7-Eleven needs to emphasize responsiveness. That group of customers expects convenience and will pay for it. On the other hand, the Sam's Club supply chain needs to focus tightly on efficiency. The Sam's Club customer is very price conscious and the supply chain needs to find every opportunity to reduce costs so that these savings can be passed on to the customers. Both of these companies' supply chains are well aligned with their business strategies and because of this they are each successful in their markets.

There are three steps to use in aligning your supply chain with your business strategy. The first step is to understand the markets that your company serves. The second step is to define the strengths or core competencies of your company and the role the company can or could play in serving its markets. The last step is to develop the needed supply chain capabilities to support the roles your company has chosen.

Understand the Markets Your Company Serves

Begin by asking questions about your customers. What kind of customer does your company serve? What kind of customer does your customer sell to? What kind of supply chain is your company a part of? The answers to these questions will tell you what supply chains your company serves and whether your supply chain needs to emphasize responsiveness or efficiency. Chopra and Meindl have defined the following attributes that help to clarify requirements for the customers you serve. These attributes are:

- *The quantity of the product needed in each lot*—Do your customers want small amounts of products or will they buy large quantities? A customer at a convenience store or a drug store buys in small quantities. A customer of a discount warehouse club, such as Sam's Club, buys in large quantities.

- *The response time that customers are willing to tolerate*—Do your customers buy on short notice and expect quick service or is a longer lead time acceptable? Customers of a fast food restaurant certainly buy on short notice and expect quick service. Customers buying custom machinery would plan the purchase in advance and expect some lead time before the product could be delivered.

- *The variety of products needed*—Are customers looking for a narrow and well-defined bundle of products or are they looking for a wide selection of different kinds of products? Customers of a fashion boutique expect a narrowly defined group of products. Customers of a "big box" discount store like Wal-Mart expect a wide variety of products to be available.

- *The service level required*—Do customers expect all products to be available for immediate delivery or will they accept partial deliveries of products and longer lead times? Customers of a music store expect to get the CD they are looking for immediately or they will go elsewhere. Customers who order a custom-built new machine tool expect to wait a while before delivery.

- *The price of the product*—How much are customers willing to pay? Some customers will pay more for convenience or high levels of service and other customers look to buy based on the lowest price they can get.

- *The desired rate of innovation in the product*—How fast are new products introduced and how long before existing products become obsolete? In products such as electronics and computers, customers expect a high rate of innovation. In other products, such as house paint, customers do not desire such a high rate of innovation.

Define Core Competencies of Your Company

The next step is to define the role that your company plays or wants to play in these supply chains. What kind of supply chain participant is your company? Is your company a producer, a distributor, a retailer, or a service provider? What does your company do to enable the supply chains that it is part of? What are the core competencies of your company? How does your company make money? The answers to these questions tell you what roles in a supply chain will be the best fit for your company.

Be aware that your company can serve multiple markets and participate in multiple supply chains. A company like W. W. Grainger serves several different markets. It sells maintenance, repair, and operating (MRO) supplies to large national account customers such as Ford and

Boeing and it also sells these supplies to small businesses and building contractors. These two different markets have different requirements as measured by the above customer attributes.

When you are serving multiple market segments, your company will need to look for ways to leverage its core competencies. Parts of these supply chains may be unique to the market segment they serve while other parts can be combined to achieve economies of scale. For example, if manufacturing is a core competency for a company, it can build a range of different products in common production facilities. Then different inventory and transportation options can be used to deliver the products to customers in different market segments.

Develop Needed Supply Chain Capabilities

Once you know what kind of markets your company serves and the role your company does or will play in the supply chains of these markets, then you can take this last step, which is to develop the supply chain capabilities needed to support the roles your company plays. This development is guided by the decisions made about the five supply chain drivers. Each of these drivers can be developed and managed to emphasize responsiveness or efficiency depending on the business requirements.

1. *Production*—This driver can be made very responsive by building factories that have a lot of excess capacity and that use flexible manufacturing techniques to produce a wide range of items. To be even more responsive, a company could do their production in many smaller plants that are close to major groups of customers so that delivery times would be shorter. If efficiency is desirable, then a company can build factories with very little excess capacity and have the factories optimized for producing a limited range of items. Further efficiency could be gained by centralizing production in large central plants to get better economies of scale.

2. *Inventory*—Responsiveness here can be had by stocking high levels of inventory for a wide range of products. Additional responsiveness can be gained by stocking products at many locations so as to have the inventory close to customers and available to them immediately. Efficiency in inventory management would call for reducing inventory levels of all items and especially of items that do not sell as frequently. Also, economies of scale and cost savings could be gotten by stocking inventory in only a few central locations.

3. *Location*—A location approach that emphasizes responsiveness would be one where a company opens up many locations to be physically close to its customer base. For example, McDonald's has used location to be very responsive to its customers by opening up lots of stores in its high volume markets. Efficiency can be achieved by operating from only a few locations and centralizing activities in common locations. An example of this is the way Dell serves large geographical markets from only a few central locations that perform a wide range of activities.

4. *Transportation*—Responsiveness can be achieved by a transportation mode that is fast and flexible. Many companies that sell products through catalogs or over the Internet are able to provide high levels of responsiveness by using transportation to deliver their products, often within 24 hours. FedEx and UPS are two companies who can provide very responsive transportation services. Efficiency can be emphasized by transporting products in larger batches and doing it less often. The use of transportation modes such as ship, rail, and pipelines can be very efficient. Transportation can be made more efficient if it is originated out of a central hub facility instead of from many branch locations.

5. *Information*—The power of this driver grows stronger each year as the technology for collecting and sharing information becomes more widespread, easier to use, and less expensive. Information, much like money, is a very useful commodity because it can be applied directly to enhance the performance of the other four supply chain drivers. High levels of responsiveness can be achieved when companies collect and share accurate and timely data generated by the operations of the other four drivers. The supply chains that serve the electronics markets are some of the most responsive in the world. Companies in these supply chains from manufacturers, to distributors, to the big retail stores collect and share data about customer demand, production schedules, and inventory levels.

Where efficiency is more the focus, less information about fewer activities can be collected. Companies may also elect to share less information among themselves so as not to risk having that information used against them. Please note, however, that these information efficiencies are only efficiencies in the short term and they become less efficient over time because the cost of information continues to drop and the cost of the other four drivers usually continues to rise. Over the longer term, those companies and supply chains that learn how to maximize the use of information to get optimal performance from the other drivers will gain the most market share and be the most profitable.

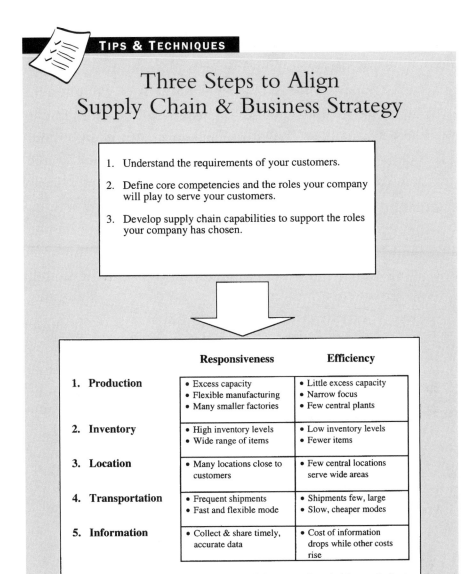

Three Steps to Align
Supply Chain & Business Strategy

1. Understand the requirements of your customers.

2. Define core competencies and the roles your company will play to serve your customers.

3. Develop supply chain capabilities to support the roles your company has chosen.

	Responsiveness	Efficiency
1. Production	• Excess capacity • Flexible manufacturing • Many smaller factories	• Little excess capacity • Narrow focus • Few central plants
2. Inventory	• High inventory levels • Wide range of items	• Low inventory levels • Fewer items
3. Location	• Many locations close to customers	• Few central locations serve wide areas
4. Transportation	• Frequent shipments • Fast and flexible mode	• Shipments few, large • Slow, cheaper modes
5. Information	• Collect & share timely, accurate data	• Cost of information drops while other costs rise

Supply chain capabilities of responsiveness and efficiency come from decisions made about the five supply chain drivers.

EXECUTIVE INSIGHT

Sunil Chopra is the IBM Distinguished Professor of Operations Management at Northwestern University's Kellogg School of Management and a director of the Masters of Management in Manufacturing program. He is also co-author of *Supply Chain Management: Strategy, Planning, and Operation*, a definitive and widely recognized source book in the field.

Wal-Mart and Dell Computers are two companies that have risen to prominence using a business strategy that offers low prices as a key selling point to their customers. This strategy requires that their supply chains be highly efficient in order to generate the cost savings needed to make a profit at the low prices they offer. Professor Chopra has followed these two companies and offers an analysis of how they have aligned their supply chains to support their business strategies.

To begin with, he points out that Wal-Mart's competitors opened stores in ones and twos and used demographic data to select store sites. Wal-Mart took a supply chain approach and would not even open a store in an area unless they determined that the area could support a distribution center (DC) and a sufficient number of stores to gain scale economies at the DC.

Then they targeted specific business operations from which to get efficiencies. "Wal-Mart said 15 years ago we are going to replenish our stores much more efficiently. They began to replenish stores two times a week where their competition was replenishing two times a month. What this meant was that a Wal-Mart manager only had to forecast for half a week and an equally capable store manager elsewhere had to forecast sales and inventory needs for half a month—they couldn't do as well.

"Since they were replenishing more often, they pioneered the cross-docking technique in order to reduce the cost of small lot replenishment. They also said that they would own and control their own trucks and their computer systems because these were the two assets that they used to make their supply chain so efficient. They invested heavily in information technology and trucks—they bought a fleet of trucks. They made these into core competencies of the company.

"When I look at Dell," said Professor Chopra, "I see a company who was able to live through and learn from a big mistake they made early on. Their roots were as a direct sales company but then in the early 90s they tried to sell through retail stores and almost went broke. That drove them back to the direct model and they have not strayed since.

"PCs are now much like cars, it is more of a replacement market than a growth market. Customers know what they want and they also want a good price. Dell's message to the market is customization and great prices. They can support this strategy because they enjoy economies of scale and postpone assembly. They use a few large facilities to assemble PCs, they assemble to order and not to stock so inventory is kept very low. In a high change technology market they do not get stuck with obsolete inventory. Their shipping costs are high but there is enough profit margin to cover that.

"This business model is finely tuned to the demands of the market, but what would happen if the PC market suddenly changed?" Professor Chopra painted a scenario that gives insight into how a company must always adjust its strategy and its supply chain to the demands of the market. "Low inventory is good in a technology market where there is a lot of churn and customers value customization. But what if the PC market is on the verge of standardization? The higher up we get in PC performance levels, the less the value of the next incremental improvement in performance. Dell and its

EXECUTIVE INSIGHT (CONTINUED)

competitors all use many of the same components to build their machines. If the market no longer values customization and simply wants the best price on a standard machine, then the Dell model doesn't work as well. Build to stock and position inventory close to the customers via retail stores becomes a better model."

There is no one right model for a supply chain. Markets change and as they do, businesses need to reevaluate their business model and their strategy. "Since a company's supply chain has a great impact on its ability to execute its business model successfully, that supply chain must always be adjusted as the business strategy changes."

Chapter Summary

A supply chain is composed of all the companies involved in the design, production, and delivery of a product to market. Supply chain management is the coordination of production, inventory, location, and transportation among the participants in a supply chain to achieve the best mix of responsiveness and efficiency for the market being served. The goal of supply chain management is to increase sales of goods and services to the final, end use customer while at the same time reducing both inventory and operating expenses.

The business model of vertical integration that came out of the industrial economy has given way to "virtual integration" of companies in a supply chain. Each company now focuses on its core competencies and partners with other companies that have complementary capabilities for the design and delivery of products to market. Companies must focus on improvements in their core competencies in order to keep up with the fast pace of market and technological change in today's economy.

To succeed in the competitive markets that make up today's economy, companies must learn to align their supply chains with the demands of the markets they serve. Supply chain performance is now a distinct competitive advantage for companies who excel in this area. One of the largest companies in North America is a testament to the power of effective supply chain management. Wal-Mart has grown steadily over the last 20 years and much, if not most, of its success is directly related to its evolving capabilities to continually improve its supply chain.

CHAPTER 2

Supply Chain Operations: Planning and Sourcing

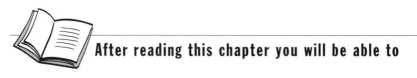

After reading this chapter you will be able to

- Gain a conceptual appreciation of the business operations in any supply chain
- Exercise an executive level understanding of operations involved in supply chain planning and sourcing
- Start to assess how well these operations are working within your own company

s the saying goes, "It's not what you know, but what you can remember when you need it." Since there is an infinite amount of detail in any situation, the trick is to find useful models that capture the salient facts and provide a framework to organize the rest of the relevant details. The purpose of this chapter is to provide some useful models of the business operations that make up the supply chain.

A Useful Model of Supply Chain Operations

In the first chapter we saw that there are five drivers of supply chain performance. These drivers can be thought of as the design parameters or policy decisions that define the shape and capabilities of any supply chain. Within the context created by these policy decisions, a supply chain goes about doing its job by performing regular, ongoing operations. These are the "nuts and bolts" operations at the core of every supply chain.

As a way to get a high level understanding of these operations and how they relate to each other, we can use the supply chain operations research or SCOR model developed by the Supply-Chain Council (Supply Chain Council Inc., 1150 Freeport Road, Pittsburgh, PA 15238, www.supply-chain.org). This model identifies four categories of operations. We will use these following four categories to organize and discuss supply chain operations:

- Plan
- Source
- Make
- Deliver

Plan

This refers to all the operations needed to plan and organize the operations in the other three categories. We will investigate three operations in this category in some detail: demand forecasting; product pricing; and inventory management.

Source

Operations in this category include the activities necessary to acquire the inputs to create products or services. We will look at two operations here. The first, procurement, is the acquisition of materials and services. The second operation, credit and collections, is not traditionally seen as a sourcing activity but it can be thought of as, literally, the acquisition of cash. Both these operations have a big impact on the efficiency of a supply chain.

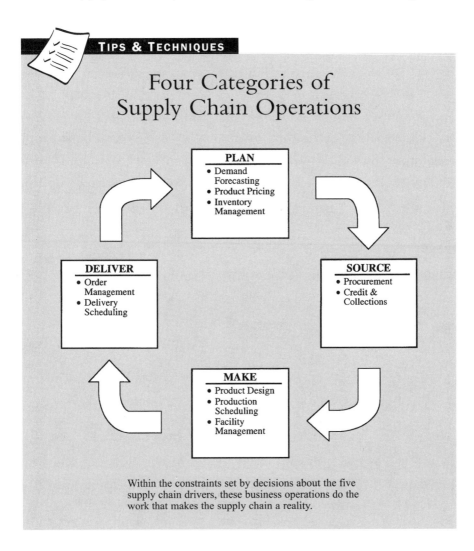

Four Categories of Supply Chain Operations

PLAN
- Demand Forecasting
- Product Pricing
- Inventory Management

SOURCE
- Procurement
- Credit & Collections

MAKE
- Product Design
- Production Scheduling
- Facility Management

DELIVER
- Order Management
- Delivery Scheduling

Within the constraints set by decisions about the five supply chain drivers, these business operations do the work that makes the supply chain a reality.

Make

This category includes the operations required to develop and build the products and services that a supply chain provides. Operations that we will discuss in this category are: product design; production management; and facility and management. The SCOR model does not specifically include the product design and development process but it is included here because it is integral to the production process.

Deliver

These operations encompass the activities that are part of receiving customer orders and delivering products to customers. The two main operations we will review are order entry/order fulfillment and product delivery. These two operations constitute the core connections between companies in a supply chain.

The rest of this chapter presents further detail in the categories of Plan and Source. There is an executive level overview of three main operations that constitute the Planning process and two operations that comprise the Sourcing process. Chapter 3 presents an executive overview of the key operations in Making and Delivering.

EXECUTIVE INSIGHT

There is also a supply operation called "adaptability." Business is an evolving set of challenges and adaptability is what a company needs in order to succeed over the long run.

Paper Enterprises (www.paperenterprises.com) is a distributor of food service and paper disposables and janitorial supplies. They are based in the Bronx and serve the entire New York metropolitan area. Herb Sedler founded the company in 1961. His son Jordan has been working in the business for over 23 years.

Success in a market like New York City calls for a company to be adept at maintaining high levels of customer service while also operating as efficiently as possible. "You learn through trial and error but you learn. This is what adaptability is all about," said Jordan Sedler. "For instance, in a lot of Manhattan buildings you have to use a freight elevator manned by a guy who may not really care about your delivery schedule. You learn to bring him a doughnut and coffee."

"In New York City there are about 300 competitors for every market segment," said Herb Sedler. "There are three or four big, overhead laden corporations and then 297 little guys running around with trucks who buy cheap and sell cheap. Paper Enterprises straddles both worlds. On the one hand, we compete with the big corporations, and on the other hand, we didn't want to compete with the little guys so we decided to make them our customers. We became a re-distributor who could buy in bulk from manufacturers and resell to all the smaller operators."

Paper Enterprises fosters a mindset of customer service in all of its staff and then they focus on the day-to-day demands of delivering that customer service. "I have set the tone that the customer is king," said Herb. "You have to have a staff who loves the challenge of satisfying the customer. In today's ABC (activity based costing) world this drive for customer satisfaction does not always look efficient. But it is the relentless dedication to satisfying the customer that ultimately pays off."

"Logistics. . . , " said Jordan, "it comes down to being able to operate under some pretty tough circumstances. There is always a problem with delivery windows—70 percent of our customers have 2 1/2 hour delivery windows that we have to meet. And the equipment you use has to fit the terrain. In lower Manhattan you just can't use trucks over a certain size. Imagine trying to back an 18 wheeler into a loading dock across four lanes of traffic with pedestrians crossing back and forth."

Jordan identified some other operating issues that require his attention. "We have a difficult time finding warehouse space. In New York it is often just not available and when it is available it costs way too much. Also in this city there is an interesting situation that you have when it comes to people. We hire people from many different ethnic and cultural backgrounds and there is a cliquish tendency in the employees from each of these cultures. It is a real trick to keep these cliques from distracting people and undermining the company environment."

When they look at technology Herb and Jordan take a very pragmatic approach. "We have two goals for using technology," said Jordan. "The first goal is to lower our cost of doing business in a measurable way. How can we use technology to lower costs in inventory control, warehouse management, and order fulfillment? The second goal is to lower our error rate. We don't want people to manually handle and re-handle data like purchase orders, invoices, etc., because it just increases the error rate. Our motto is 'Get it right the first time.'"

"We also want to bring technology to our customer base," added Herb. "The immigrants are the new entrepreneurs. They have no formal training in distribution and they are often one-man shows. I am a mentor in the Baruch College entrepreneurship program. As they succeed, Paper Enterprises will succeed. As we show them technology and practices that help them grow, we become a logistics organization and not just a paper distributor."

"I learn something every day. Running a business in New York is like working in a microcosm of the whole world. People from every country are here," said Jordan. "And it's funny, where you may think that there would be intense and cutthroat competition—not so—there has evolved a cooperative spirit. That is an important part of how we do business." "After 9/11," said Herb, "we called a meeting of distributors in the city and said we would make our trucks available to our competitors who needed to get into lower Manhattan if they would help us in New Jersey." Adaptability is an ever-changing blend of competition and cooperation.

Demand Forecasting (Plan)

Supply chain management decisions are based on forecasts that define which products will be required, what amount of these products will be called for, and when they will be needed. The demand forecast becomes the basis for companies to plan their internal operations and to cooperate among each other to meet market demand.

All forecasts deal with four major variables that combine to determine what market conditions will be like. Those variables are:

1. Demand

2. Supply

3. Product Characteristics

4. Competitive Environment

Demand refers to the overall market demand for a group of related products or services. Is the market growing or declining? If so, what is the yearly or quarterly rate of growth or decline? Or maybe the market is relatively mature and demand is steady at a level that has been predictable for some period of years. Also, many products have a seasonal demand pattern. For example, snow skis and heating oil are more in demand in the winter and tennis rackets and sun screen are more in demand in the summer. Perhaps the market is a developing market—the products or services are new and there is not much historical data on demand or the demand varies widely because new customers are just being introduced to the products. Markets where there is little historical data and lots of variability are the most difficult when it comes to demand forecasting.

Supply is determined by the number of producers of a product and by the lead times that are associated with a product. The more producers there are of a product and the shorter the lead times, the more predictable this variable is. When there are only a few suppliers or when lead times are longer, there is more potential uncertainty in a market. Like variability in demand, uncertainty in supply makes forecasting more difficult. Also, longer lead times associated with a product require a longer time horizon over which forecasts must be done. Supply chain forecasts must cover a time period that encompasses the combined lead times of all the components that go into the creation of a final product.

Product characteristics include the features of a product that influence customer demand for the product. Is the product new and developing quickly like many electronic products or is the product mature and changing slowly or not at all, as is the case with many commodity products? Forecasts for mature products can cover longer timeframes than forecasts for products that are developing quickly. It is also important to know whether a product will steal demand away from another product. Can it be substituted for another product? Or will the use of a product drive the complementary use of a related product? Products that either compete with or complement each other should be forecasted together.

Competitive environment refers to the actions of a company and its competitors. What is the market share of a company? Regardless of whether the total size of a market is growing or shrinking, what is the trend in an individual company's market share? Is it growing or declining? What is the market share trend of competitors? Market share trends can be influenced by product promotions and price wars, so forecasts should take into account such events that are planned for the upcoming period. Forecasts should also account for anticipated promotions and price wars that will be initiated by competitors.

Forecasting Methods

There are four basic methods to use when doing forecasts. Most forecasts are done using various combinations of these four methods. Chopra and Meindl define these methods as:

1. Qualitative

2. Causal

3. Time Series

4. Simulation

Qualitative methods rely upon a person's intuition or subjective opinions about a market. These methods are most appropriate when there is little historical data to work with. When a new line of products is introduced, people can make forecasts based on comparisons with other products or situations that they consider similar. People can forecast using production adoption curves that they feel reflect what will happen in the market.

Causal methods of forecasting assume that demand is strongly related to particular environmental or market factors. For instance, demand for commercial loans is often closely correlated to interest rates. So if interest rate cuts are expected in the next period of time, then loan forecasts can be derived using a causal relationship with interest rates. Another strong causal relationship exists between price and demand. If prices are lowered, demand can be expected to increase and if prices are raised, demand can be expected to fall.

Time series methods are the most common form of forecasting. They are based on the assumption that historical patterns of demand are a good indicator of future demand. These methods are best when there is a reliable body of historical data and the markets being forecast are stable and have demand patterns that do not vary much from one year to the next. Mathematical techniques such as moving averages and exponential smoothing are used to create forecasts based on time series data. These techniques are employed by most forecasting software packages.

Simulation methods use combinations of causal and time series methods to imitate the behavior of consumers under different circumstances. This method can be used to answer questions such as what will happen to revenue if prices on a line of products are lowered or what will happen to market share if a competitor introduces a competing product or opens a store nearby.

Few companies use only one of these methods to do forecasts. Most companies do several forecasts using several methods and then combine the results of these different forecasts into the actual forecast that they use to plan their business. Studies have shown that this process of creating forecasts using different methods and then combining the results into a final forecast usually produces better accuracy than the output of any one method alone.

Regardless of the forecasting methods used, when doing forecasts and evaluating their results it is important to keep several things in mind. First of all, short-term forecasts are inherently more accurate than long-term forecasts. The effect of business trends and conditions can be much more accurately calculated over short periods than over longer periods. When Wal-Mart began restocking its stores twice a week instead of twice a month, the store managers were able to significantly increase the accuracy of their forecasts because the time periods involved dropped from two or three weeks to three or four days. Most long range, multi-year forecasts are highly speculative.

Aggregate forecasts are more accurate than forecasts for individual products or for small market segments. For example, annual forecasts for soft drink sales in a given metropolitan area are fairly accurate but when these forecasts are broken down to sales by districts within the metropolitan area, they become less accurate. Aggregate forecasts are made using a broad base of data that provides good forecasting accuracy. As a rule, the more narrowly focused or specific a forecast is, the less data is available and the more variability there is in the data, so the accuracy is diminished.

Finally, forecasts are always wrong to a greater or lesser degree. There are no perfect forecasts and businesses need to assign some expected degree of error to every forecast. An accurate forecast may have a degree of error that is plus or minus 5 percent. A more speculative forecast may have a plus or minus 20 percent degree of error. It is important to know the degree of error because a business must have contingency plans to cover those outcomes. What would a company do if raw material prices were 5 percent higher than expected? What would it do if demand was 20 percent higher than expected?

TIPS & TECHNIQUES

The Four Forecasting Variables and the Four Forecasting Methods

Forecasting VARIABLES		
1.	Demand	Overall market demand for product
2.	Supply	Amount of product available
3.	Product Characteristics	Product features that influence demand
4.	Competitive Environment	Actions of product suppliers in the market

Forecasting METHODS		
1.	Qualitative	Relies on a person's intuition or opinions
2.	Causal	Assumes that demand is strongly related to certain factors
3.	Time Series	Based on historical demand patterns
4.	Simulation	Combines causal and time series methods

Aggregate Planning

Once demand forecasts have been created, the next step is to create a plan for the company to meet the expected demand. This is called aggregate planning and its purpose is to satisfy demand in a way that maximizes profit for the company. The planning is done at the aggregate level and not at the level of individual stock keeping units (SKUs). It sets the optimum levels of production and inventory that will be followed over the next 3 to 18 months.

The aggregate plan becomes the framework within which short-term decisions are made about production, inventory, and distribution. Production decisions involve setting parameters such as the rate of production and the amount of production capacity to use, the size of the workforce, and how much overtime and subcontracting to use. Inventory decisions include how much demand will be met immediately by inventory on hand and how much demand can be satisfied later and turned into backlogged orders. Distribution decisions define how and when product will be moved from the place of production to the place where it will be used or purchased by customers.

There are three basic approaches to take in creating the aggregate plan. They involve trade-offs among three variables. Those variables are: 1) amount of production capacity; 2) the level of utilization of the production capacity; and 3) the amount of inventory to carry. We will look briefly at each of these three approaches. In actual practice, most companies create aggregate plans that are a combination of these three approaches.

1. *Use production capacity to match demand.* In this approach the total amount of production capacity is matched to the level of demand. The objective here is to use 100 percent of capacity at all times. This is achieved by adding or eliminating plant capacity as needed and hiring and laying off employees as needed. This approach results in low levels of inventory but it can be very expensive to

implement if the cost of adding or reducing plant capacity is high. It is also often disruptive and demoralizing to the workforce if people are constantly being hired or fired as demand rises and falls. This approach works best when the cost of carrying inventory is high and the cost of changing capacity—plant and workforce—is low.

2. *Utilize varying levels of total capacity to match demand.* This approach can be used if there is excess production capacity available. If existing plants are not used 24 hours a day and 7 days a week then there is an opportunity to meet changing demand by increasing or decreasing utilization of production capacity. The size of the workforce can be maintained at a steady rate and overtime and flexible work scheduling used to match production rates. The result is low levels of inventory and also lower average levels of capacity utilization. The approach makes sense when the cost of carrying inventory is high and the cost of excess capacity is relatively low.

3. *Use inventory and backlogs to match demand.* Using this approach provides for stability in the plant capacity and workforce and enables a constant rate of output. Production is not matched with demand. Instead inventory is either built up during periods of low demand in anticipation of future demand or inventory is allowed to run low and backlogs are built up in one period to be filled in a following period. This approach results in higher capacity utilization and lower costs of changing capacity but it does generate large inventories and backlogs over time as demand fluctuates. It should be used when the cost of capacity and changing capacity is high and the cost of carrying inventory and backlogs is relatively low.

Product Pricing (Plan)

Companies and entire supply chains can influence demand over time by using price. Depending on how price is used, it will tend to either maximize revenue or gross profit. Typically marketing and sales people want to make pricing decisions that will stimulate demand during peak seasons. The aim here is to maximize total revenue. Often financial or production people want to make pricing decisions that stimulate demand during low periods. Their aim is to maximize gross profit in peak demand periods and generate revenue to cover costs during low demand periods.

Relationship of Cost Structure to Pricing

The question for each company to ask is, "Is it better to do price promotion during peak periods to increase revenue or during low periods to cover costs?" The answer depends on the company's cost structure. If a company has flexibility to vary the size of its workforce and productive capacity and the cost of carrying inventory is high, then it is best to create more demand in peak seasons. If there is less flexibility to vary workforce and capacity and if cost to carry inventory is low, it is best to create demand in low periods.

An example of a company that can quickly ramp up production would be an electronics components manufacturer. Such companies have invested in plant and equipment that can be quickly reconfigured to produce different final products from an inventory of standard component parts. The finished goods inventory is expensive to carry because it soon becomes obsolete and must be written off.

These companies are generally motivated to run promotions in peak periods to stimulate demand even further. Since they can quickly increase production levels, a reduction in the profit margin can be made up for by an increase in total sales if they are able to sell all the product that they manufacture.

A company that cannot quickly ramp up production levels is a paper mill. The plant and equipment involved in making paper is very expensive and requires a long lead time to build. Once in place, a paper mill operates most efficiently if it is able to run at a steady rate all year long. The cost of carrying an inventory of paper products is less expensive

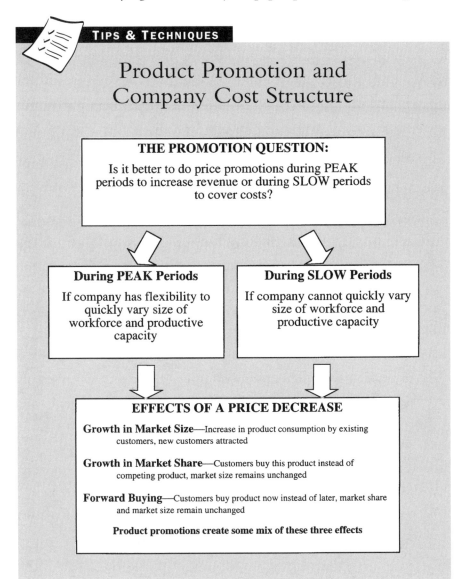

TIPS & TECHNIQUES

Product Promotion and Company Cost Structure

THE PROMOTION QUESTION:

Is it better to do price promotions during PEAK periods to increase revenue or during SLOW periods to cover costs?

During PEAK Periods

If company has flexibility to quickly vary size of workforce and productive capacity

During SLOW Periods

If company cannot quickly vary size of workforce and productive capacity

EFFECTS OF A PRICE DECREASE

Growth in Market Size—Increase in product consumption by existing customers, new customers attracted

Growth in Market Share—Customers buy this product instead of competing product, market size remains unchanged

Forward Buying—Customers buy product now instead of later, market share and market size remain unchanged

Product promotions create some mix of these three effects

than carrying an inventory of electronic components because paper products are commodity items that will not become obsolete. These products also can be stored in less expensive warehouse facilities and are less likely to be stolen.

A paper mill is motivated to do price promotions in periods of low demand. In periods of high demand the focus is on maintaining a good profit margin. Since production levels cannot be increased anyway, there is no way to respond to or profit from an increase in demand. In periods where demand is below the available production level, then there is value in increased demand. The fixed cost of the plant and equipment is constant so it is best to try to balance demand with available production capacity. This way the plant can be run steadily at full capacity.

Inventory Management (Plan)

Inventory management is a set of techniques that are used to manage the inventory levels within different companies in a supply chain. The aim is to reduce the cost of inventory as much as possible while still maintaining the service levels that customers require. Inventory management takes its major inputs from the demand forecasts for products and the prices of products. With these two inputs, inventory management is an ongoing process of balancing product inventory levels to meet demand and exploiting economies of scale to get the best product prices.

As we discussed in Chapter 1, there are three kinds of inventory: 1) cycle inventory; 2) seasonal inventory; and 3) safety inventory. Cycle inventory and seasonal inventory are both influenced by economy of scale considerations. The cost structure of the companies in any supply chain will suggest certain levels of inventory based on production costs and inventory carrying cost. Safety inventory is influenced by the predictability of product demand. The less predictable product demand is, the higher the level of safety inventory is required to cover unexpected swings in demand.

The inventory management operation in a company or an entire supply chain is composed of a blend of activities related to managing the three different types of inventory. Each type of inventory has its own specific challenges and the mix of these challenges will vary from one company to another and from one supply chain to another.

Cycle Inventory

Cycle inventory is the inventory required to meet product demand over the time period between placing orders for the product. Cycle inventory exists because economies of scale make it desirable to make fewer orders of large quantities of a product rather than continuous orders of small product quantity. The end use customer of a product may actually use a product in continuous small amounts throughout the year. But the distributor and the manufacturer of that product may find it more cost efficient to produce and stock the product in large batches that do not match the usage pattern.

Cycle inventory is the buildup of inventory in the supply chain due to the fact that production and stocking of inventory is done in lot sizes that are larger than the ongoing demand for the product. For example, a distributor may experience an ongoing demand for Item A that is 100 units per week. The distributor finds, however, that it is most cost effective to order in batches of 650 units. Every six weeks or so the distributor places an order causing cycle inventory to build up in the distributor's warehouse at the beginning of the ordering period. The manufacturer of Item A that all the distributors order from may find that it is most efficient for them to manufacture in batches of 14,000 units at a time. This also results in the buildup of cycle inventory at the manufacturer's location.

Economic Order Quantity

Given the cost structure of a company, there is an order quantity that is the most cost effective amount to purchase at a time. This is called the economic order quantity (EOQ) and it is calculated as:

$$EOQ = \sqrt{\frac{2UO}{hC}} \quad \text{(square root of 2UO / hC)}$$

where:

U = annual usage rate

O = ordering cost

C = cost per unit

h = holding cost per year as a percentage of unit cost

For instance, let's say that Item Z has an annual usage rate (U) of 240, a fixed cost per order (O) of \$5.00, a unit cost (C) of \$7.00, and an annual holding cost (h) of 30 percent per unit. If we do the math, it works out as:

$$EOQ = \sqrt{\frac{2 \times 240 \times 5.00}{.30 \times 7.00}}$$

$$EOQ = \sqrt{\frac{2400}{2.1}}$$

$$EOQ = \sqrt{1142.86}$$

EOQ = 33.81 and rounded to the nearest whole unit, it is 34

If the annual usage rate for Item Z is 240, then the monthly usage rate is 20. An EOQ of 34 represents about 1 and 3/4 months supply. This may not be a convenient order size. Small changes in the EOQ do not have a big impact on total ordering and holding costs so it is best to round off the EOQ quantity to the nearest standard ordering size. In the case of Item Z, there may be 30 units in a case. So it would make sense to adjust the EOQ for Item Z to 30.

The EOQ formula works to calculate an order quantity that results in the most efficient investment of money in inventory. Efficiency here is defined as the lowest total unit cost for each inventory item. If a certain inventory item has a high usage rate and it is expensive, the EOQ formula recommends a low order quantity which results in more orders per year but less money invested in each order. If another inventory

TIPS & TECHNIQUES

Understanding the
Economic Ordering Quantity (EOQ)

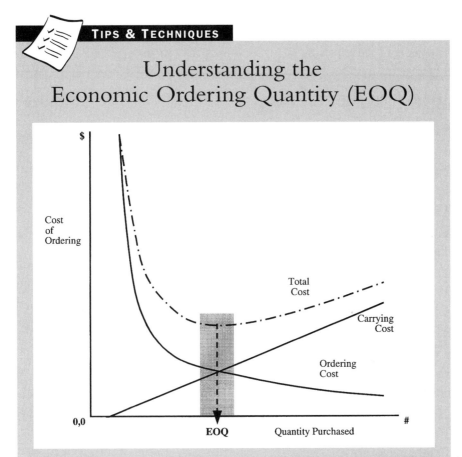

Good inventory management requires a company to know the EOQ for all the products it buys. The EOQ for different products changes over time so a company needs an ongoing measurement process to keep the numbers accurate and up to date.

item has a low usage rate and it is inexpensive, the EOQ formula recommends a high order quantity. This means fewer orders per year but since the unit cost is low, it still results in the most efficient amount of money to invest in that item.

Seasonal Inventory

Seasonal inventory happens when a company or a supply chain with a fixed amount of productive capacity decides to produce and stockpile products in anticipation of future demand. If future demand is going to exceed productive capacity, then the answer is to produce products in times of low demand that can be put into inventory to meet the high demand in the future.

Decisions about seasonal inventory are driven by a desire to get the best economies of scale given the capacity and cost structure of each company in the supply chain. If it is expensive for a manufacturer to increase productive capacity, then capacity can be considered as fixed. Once the annual demand for the manufacturer's products is determined, the most efficient schedule to utilize that fixed capacity can be calculated.

This schedule will call for seasonal inventory. Managing seasonal inventory calls for demand forecasts to be accurate since large amounts of inventory can be built up this way and it can become obsolete or holding costs can mount if the inventory is not sold off as anticipated. Managing seasonal inventory also calls for manufacturers to offer price incentives to persuade distributors to purchase it and put it in their warehouses well before demand for it occurs.

Safety Inventory

Safety inventory is necessary to compensate for the uncertainty that exists in a supply chain. Retailers and distributors do not want to run out of inventory in the face of unexpected customer demand or unexpected

TIPS & TECHNIQUES

Key Points to Remember about Inventory Management

Economic Order Quantity (EOQ)

The ordering quantity of a product that minimizes both the ordering cost and the carrying cost

---

THREE KINDS OF INVENTORY

1. **Cycle Inventory**—Needed to meet product demand between normally scheduled orders

2. **Seasonal Inventory**—Produced and stockpiled in anticipation of future demand

3. **Safety Inventory**—Necessary to compensate for demand uncertainty and order lead times

---

FOUR WAYS TO REDUCE SAFTEY INVENTORY

1. **Reduce Demand Uncertainty**—Learn to do better product demand forecasts

2. **Reduce Order Lead Times**—Shorter lead times mean less safety inventory needed for coverage

3. **Reduce Lead Time Variability**—Further reduces need for safety inventory

4. **Reduce Availability Uncertainty**—Ensure product availability when demand occurs

---

delay in receiving replenishment orders so they keep safety stock on hand. As a rule, the higher the level of uncertainty, the higher the level of safety stock that is required.

Safety inventory for an item can be defined as the amount of inventory on hand for an item when the next replenishment EOQ lot arrives. This means that the safety stock is inventory that does not turn over. In effect, it becomes a fixed asset and it drives up the cost of carrying inventory. Companies need to find a balance between their desire to carry a wide range of products and offer high availability on all of them and their conflicting desire to keep the cost of inventory as low as possible. That balance is reflected quite literally in the amount of safety stock that a company carries.

Procurement (Source)

Traditionally, the main activities of a purchasing manager were to beat up potential suppliers on price and then buy products from the lowest cost supplier that could be found. That is still an important activity, but there are other activities that are becoming equally important. Because of this the purchasing activity is now seen as part of a broader function called procurement. The procurement function can be broken into five main activity categories:

1. Purchasing
2. Consumption Management
3. Vendor Selection
4. Contract Negotiation
5. Contract Management

Purchasing

These activities are the routine activities related to issuing purchase orders for needed products. There are two types of products that a

EXECUTIVE INSIGHT

Service means different things to different customers. Customers have needs that vary depending on their strengths and weaknesses and the business models that they use. Effective supply chain companies learn to tailor their service offerings to match the individual customer's needs.

Service Paper Company (www.servicepaper.com) distributes retail food and foodservice products, industrial packaging, healthcare disposables, and janitorial supplies. They have been in business since 1937 and have locations in Seattle, Portland, and Spokane. Leonard Green is Service Paper's president.

"We have customers in a number of different market segments and these customers are in different stages of their business growth," Leonard said. "We look at each customer and strive to provide a mix of products and services that will make us a valuable part of their operations. Let me illustrate this with an example of a customer that we have served for some time now and through several stages in their growth. Back in the '80s we began doing business with a small company that operated a handful of coffee shops in Seattle.

"This small company insisted on using specially made products featuring their logo. Their original supplier was not willing to stock "special print" inventory. At Service Paper we viewed the request as a customer requirement rather than an inconvenience. We began taking large shipments of their logoed special print items from various manufacturers and distributed these products to their coffee shops several times a week.

"They were growing rapidly and we were able to work with their staff to facilitate the procurement of their foodservice disposables. We knew the products and the manufacturers in the foodservice industry so we were able to help in educating their purchasing people and in suggesting the products they needed. We also helped them with sourcing and even in scheduling production runs with manufacturers for products they needed.

"Early on the company CEO was very hands-on in all of these areas. He knew what he wanted the company to be and he was intent on finding the products they needed. We steered him to the maker of a new coffee cup lid called the traveler lid. It allowed a person to sip hot coffee while they walked or drove without getting too much in their mouth all at once. When he saw the lid he liked it so much that he insisted the manufacturer give them an exclusive on the product. The manufacturer wasn't willing to do that and was ready to walk away from the business because of that demand. Since I knew both parties, I was able to act as a referee. I encouraged the CEO to see that he had a strong potential partner there and perhaps he could reconsider his position. I helped them start a business relationship that has been very beneficial to both companies ever since."

As the company expanded out of the Seattle area, Service Paper introduced them to Network Services Company. Network Services is a national cooperative of distribution companies of which Service Paper is both a member and an owner. "We got Network Services involved when the company told us they were going to expand into Chicago. I became their advocate within Network. We had lots of business in Seattle but, at first, there were only a few stores in Chicago. The Network member in Chicago was reluctant to stock the specially printed products and do the many small deliveries to the coffee shops. Then they expanded into San Francisco and I had to work hard to explain to our member there why it was a good deal.

"We had to change our operating policies to meet the customer's needs. We had to carry a substantial inventory of proprietary items and we had to accept orders that were often much smaller than our usual minimum orders. But, over time, they established credibility with us because they met their new store roll out plans and the promised volume did materialize. There are now some 25 Network members who support them nationwide."

company buys; 1) direct or strategic materials that are needed to produce the products that the company sells to its customers; and 2) indirect or MRO (maintenance, repair, and operations) products that a company consumes as part of daily operations.

The mechanics of purchasing both types of products are largely the same. Purchasing decisions are made, purchase orders are issued, vendors are contacted, and orders are placed. There is a lot of data communicated in this process between the buyer and the supplier—items and quantities ordered, prices, delivery dates, delivery addresses, billing addresses, and payment terms. One of the greatest challenges of the purchasing activity is to see to it that this data communication happens in a timely manner and without error. Much of this activity is very predictable and follows well defined routines.

Consumption Management

Effective procurement begins with an understanding of how much of what categories of products are being bought across the entire company as well as by each operating unit. There must be an understanding of how much of what kinds of products are bought from whom and at what prices.

Expected levels of consumption for different products at the various locations of a company should be set and then compared against actual consumption on a regular basis. When consumption is significantly above or below expectations, this should be brought to the attention of the appropriate parties so possible causes can be investigated and appropriate actions taken. Consumption above expectations is either a problem to be corrected or it reflects inaccurate expectations that need to be reset. Consumption below expectations may point to an opportunity that should be exploited or it also may simply reflect inaccurate expectations to begin with.

Vendor Selection

There must be an ongoing process to define the procurement capabilities needed to support the company's business plan and its operating model. This definition will provide insight into the relative importance of vendor capabilities. The value of these capabilities have to be considered in addition to simply the price of a vendor's product. The value of product quality, service levels, just in time delivery, and technical support can only be estimated in light of what is called for by the business plan and the company's operating model.

Once there is an understanding of the current purchasing situation and an appreciation of what a company needs to support its business plan and operating model, a search can be made for suppliers who have both the products and the service capabilities needed. As a general rule, a company seeks to narrow down the number of suppliers it does business with. This way it can leverage its purchasing power with a few suppliers and get better prices in return for purchasing higher volumes of product.

Contract Negotiation

As particular business needs arise, contracts must be negotiated with individual vendors on the preferred vendor list. This is where the specific items, prices, and service levels are worked out. The simplest negotiations are for contracts to purchase indirect products where suppliers are selected on the basis of lowest price. The most complex negotiations are for contracts to purchase direct materials that must meet exacting quality requirements and where high service levels and technical support are needed.

Increasingly, though, even negotiations for the purchase of indirect items such as office supplies and janitorial products are becoming more complicated because they fall within a company's overall business plan to gain greater efficiencies in purchasing and inventory management.

Suppliers of both direct and indirect products need a common set of capabilities. Gaining greater purchasing efficiencies requires that suppliers of these products have the capabilities to set up electronic connections for purposes of receiving orders, sending delivery notifications, sending invoices, and receiving payments. Better inventory management requires that inventory levels be reduced, which often means suppliers need to make more frequent and smaller deliveries and orders must be filled accurately and completely.

All these requirements need to be negotiated in addition to the basic issues of products and prices. The negotiations must make tradeoffs between the unit price of a product and all the other value added services that are required. These other services can either be paid for by a higher margin in the unit price, or by separate payments, or by some combination of the two. Performance targets must be specified and penalties and other fees defined when performance targets are not met.

Contract Management

Once contracts are in place, vendor performance against these contracts must be measured and managed. Because companies are narrowing down their base of suppliers, the performance of each supplier that is chosen becomes more important. A particular supplier may be the only source of a whole category of products that a company needs and if it is not meeting its contractual obligations, the activities that depend on those products will suffer.

A company needs the ability to track the performance of its suppliers and hold them accountable to meet the service levels they agreed to in their contract. Just as with consumption management, people in a company need to routinely collect data about the performance of suppliers. Any supplier that consistently falls below requirements should be made aware of their shortcomings and asked to correct them.

Often the supplier themselves should be given responsibility for tracking their own performance. They should be able to proactively take action to keep their performance up to contracted levels. An example of this is the concept of vendor managed inventory (VMI). VMI calls for the vendor to monitor the inventory levels of its product within a customer's business. The vendor is responsible for watching usage rates and calculating EOQs. The vendor proactively ships products to the customer locations that need them and invoices the customer for those shipments under terms defined in the contract.

Credit and Collections (Source)

Procurement is the sourcing process a company uses to get the goods and services it needs. Credit and collections is the sourcing process that a company uses to get its money. The credit operation screens potential customers to make sure the company only does business with customers who will be able to pay their bills. The collections operation is what actually brings in the money that the company has earned.

Approving a sale is like making a loan for the sale amount for a length of time defined by the payment terms. Good credit management tries to fulfill customer demand for products and also minimize the amount of money tied up in receivables. This is analogous to the way good inventory management strives to meet customer demand and also minimize the amount of money tied up in inventory.

The supply chains that a company participates in are often selected on the basis of credit decisions. Much of the trust and cooperation that is possible between companies who do business together is based upon good credit ratings and timely payments of invoices. Credit decisions affect who a company will sell to and also the terms of the sale. The credit and collections function can be broken into three main categories of activity:

1. Set Credit Policy

2. Implement Credit and Collections Practices

3. Manage Credit Risk

Set Credit Policy

Credit policy is set by senior managers in a company such as the controller, chief financial officer, treasurer, and chief executive officer. The first step in this process is to review the performance of the company's receivables. Every company has defined a set of measurements that they use to analyze their receivables, such as: days sales outstanding (DSO); percent of receivables past customer payment terms; and bad debt write-off amount as percent of sales. What are the trends? Where are there problems?

Once management has an understanding of the company's receivables situation and the trends affecting that situation, they can take the next step which is to set or change risk acceptance criteria to respond to the state of the company's receivables. These criteria should change over time as economic and market conditions evolve. These criteria define the kinds of credit risks that the company will take with different kinds of customers and the payment terms that will be offered.

Implement Credit and Collections Practices

These activities involve putting in place and operating the procedures that will carry out and enforce the credit policies of the company. The first major activity in this category is to work with the company salespeople to approve sales to specific customers. As noted earlier, making a sale is like making a loan for the amount of the sale. Customers often buy from a company because that company extends them larger lines of credit and longer payment terms than its competitors. Credit analysis goes a long way to assure that this loan is only made to customers who will pay it off promptly as called for by the terms of the sale.

After a sale is made, people in the credit area work with customers to provide various kinds of service. They work with customers to process product returns and issue credit memos for returned products. They work with customers to resolve disputes and clear up questions by providing copies of contracts, purchase orders, and invoices.

The third major activity that is performed is collections. This is a process that starts with the ongoing maintenance of each customer's accounts payable status. Customers that have past due accounts are contacted and payments are requested. Sometimes new payment terms and schedules are negotiated.

The collections activity also includes the work necessary to receive and process customer payments that can come in a variety of different forms. Some customers will wish to pay by electronic funds transfer (EFT). Others will use bank drafts and revolving lines of credit or purchasing cards. If customers are in other countries there are still other ways that payment can be made, such as international letters of credit.

Manage Credit Risk

The credit function works to help the company take intelligent risks that support its business plan. What may be a bad credit decision from one perspective may be a good business decision from another perspective. If a company wants to gain market share in a certain area it may make credit decisions that help it to do so. Credit people work with other people in the business to find innovative ways to lower the risk of selling to new kinds of customers.

Managing risk can be accomplished by creating credit programs that are tailored to the needs of customers in certain market segments such as high technology companies, start-up companies, construction contractors, or customers in foreign countries. Payment terms that are attractive to customers in these market segments can be devised. Credit risks can be lowered by the use of credit insurance, liens on customer assets, and government loan guarantees for exports.

For important customers and particularly large individual sales, people in the credit area work with others in the company to structure special deals just for a single customer. This increases the value that the company can provide to such a customer and can be a significant part of securing important new business.

EXECUTIVE INSIGHT

Building a recognized and valued brand name is a goal that many companies try to accomplish. Doing this calls for a company to be adaptable, to tailor its services to customers' needs, and to achieve high levels of efficiency in the other supply chain operations that it performs.

Waxie Sanitary Supply (www.waxie.com) is a distributor with locations throughout California, Nevada, Utah, Colorado, and Arizona. Over the last 20 years they have been very successful in developing and promoting Waxie brand name products. Charles Wax is the CEO and Cliff Robbins is the company's Director of Information Technology.

Charles Wax explained that, "The company was founded in 1945 by my uncle Harry Wax and then my father Morris joined him soon after. The company started under the name of San Diego Janitorial Supply. We grew and in 1962 bought another company in southern California named Kleenline. We kept both names because each had a loyal customer base. In the 1980s we expanded out of the southern California area and we felt the need for a new company name that would convey who we were as we entered new markets.

"Uncle Harry was a Seabee in the navy during World War II. In the navy he got the nickname "Waxie" and the logo he chose when he first started the company was a bee operating a floor waxing machine. So it seemed natural for us to adopt the name Waxie and to use a bee as our logo.

"We wanted to develop our own brand name because a lot of companies buy product and then forget where they bought it. If we put our name on the product they would remember where they got it. Also, if they like the product then they have to come to us to buy it. We redesigned and standardized our logo and the company slogan and put them on products, forms, trucks, brochures, everything."

The first step is to create a brand name and the next step is to sell its benefits to customers. "We sell a lot of value added services," said Charles. "We educate the customer to use the best product for their specific needs. We show them how to use dilution control to optimize usage rates for chemicals. We show them how to use floor machines to cut labor costs. We train the customer's people in how to use our products.

"It is easy for a competitor of ours to say, "We have the same item and at a lower price." We respond to this by educating customers to the fact that 10 percent of their cost is product and the other 90 percent is labor. We can show them how to use our products to cut their labor costs and that's where they will see the big savings.

"We are always looking for ways to solve our customers' problems. We work with each customer to customize our service offerings for them. For instance, we did a lot of work at the Salt Lake City Olympics. To meet their delivery schedules, we got our drivers security clearance and worked closely with people running the event to bring our trucks in at night where and when they wanted them."

"We use technology to help us deliver the services that build the Waxie brand," Cliff Robbins said. "There is a system to help us do regular surveys of customers and people who aren't our customers to identify their needs and spot market trends. We equip our sales and service people in the field with laptops. They have the same access to information as they would if they were in the office—complete customer profiles, credit status, open issues, and sales history."

"There is now a web-based order entry system that lets customers view their own customized product catalogs and prices," Cliff continued. "We are working with the sales people to train our customers to use this system." Charles added that, "There is great benefit to the customers. They can order 24 by 7, they can make up their own order guides, they can see product pictures, and they can see usage information. As customers start using the system, it cuts our cost to handle the orders and we are also seeing an increase in the average order size from these customers."

Delivering the value that makes up the Waxie brand requires a coordinated effort from everyone in the company. "To focus everyone on pulling together to build the value of the Waxie brand, we track a few simple performance measures," explained Charles. "Gross margin percent measures the productivity of the sales process and gross margin growth measures the overall growth of the company. We have a program we call "All Sell All Grow." It is the bonus program for all non-sales people. We post branch and overall company gross margin growth every month throughout the company. So all employees know how we are doing and how they stand on their yearly bonus."

"Having our own brand helps us manage our margins. It insulates us somewhat from the actions of the national brand name manufacturers," observed Charles. "We wanted to create a brand that stands for who we are. To remind us why we are here and to remind customers of our value."

Chapter Summary

The business operations that drive the supply chain can be grouped into four major categories: 1) Plan; 2) Source; 3) Make; and 4) Deliver. The business operations that comprise these categories are the day-to-day operations that determine how well the supply chain works. Companies must continually make improvements in these areas.

Planning refers to all the operations needed to plan and organize the operations in the other three categories. This includes operations such as demand forecasting, product pricing, and inventory management. Increasingly, it is these planning operations that determine the potential efficiency of the supply chain.

Sourcing includes the activities necessary to acquire the inputs to create products or services. This includes operations such as procurement and credit and collections. Both these operations have a big impact on the efficiency of a supply chain.

CHAPTER 3

Supply Chain Operations: Making and Delivering

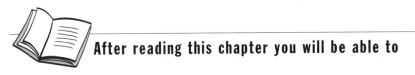

After reading this chapter you will be able to

- Exercise an executive level understanding of operations involved in the categories of making products and delivering products

- Assess supply operations in your company that may be candidates for outsourcing

Many companies and the supply chains they participate in serve customers who are growing more sophisticated every year and demanding higher levels of service. Continuous improvements to the operations described in this chapter are needed to deliver the efficiency and responsiveness that evolving supply chains require.

Product Design (Make)

Product designs and selections of the components needed to build these products are based on the technology available and product performance requirements. Until recently, little thought was given to how the design of a product and the selection of its components affect the supply chain required to make the product. Yet these costs can become 50 percent or more of the product's cost.

When considering product design from a supply chain perspective the aim is to design products with fewer parts, simple designs, and modular construction from generic sub-assemblies. This way the parts can be obtained from a small group of preferred suppliers. Inventory can be kept in the form of generic sub-assemblies at appropriate locations in the supply chain. There will not be the need to hold large finished goods inventories because customer demand can be met quickly by assembling final products from generic sub-assemblies as customer orders arrive.

The supply chain required to support a product is molded by the product's design. The more flexible, responsive, and cost efficient the supply chain, the more likely the product will succeed in its market. To illustrate this point, consider the following scenario.

Fantastic Company designs a fantastic new home entertainment system with wide screen TV and surround sound. It performs to demanding specifications and delivers impressive results. But the electronics that power the entertainment center are built with components from 12 different suppliers.

Demand takes off and the company ramps up production. Managing quality control and delivery schedules for 12 suppliers is a challenge. More procurement managers and staff are hired. Assembly of the components is complex and delays in the delivery of components from any of the suppliers can slow down production rates. So buffer stocks of finished goods are kept to compensate for this.

Several new suppliers were required to provide the specified product components. One of them has quality control problems and has to be replaced and another supplier decides after several months to cease production of the component it supplies to Fantastic Company. They bring out a new component with similar features but not an exact replacement.

Fantastic Company has to suspend production of the home entertainment system while a team of engineers redesigns the part of the system that used the discontinued component so that it can use the new component. During this time, buffer stocks run out in some locations and sales are lost when customers go elsewhere.

A competitor called Nimble Company is attracted by the success of Fantastic Company and comes out with a competing product. Nimble Company designed a product with fewer parts and uses components from only four suppliers. The cost of procurement is much lower since they only have to coordinate four suppliers instead of 12. There are no production delays due to lack of component parts and product assembly is easier.

While Fantastic Company, who pioneered the market, struggles with a balky supply chain, Nimble Company provides the market with lower cost and more reliable supply of the product. Nimble Company with its responsive and less costly supply chain takes market share away from Fantastic Company.

What can be learned here? Product design defines the shape of the supply chain and this has a great impact on the cost and availability of the product. If product design, procurement, and manufacturing people can work together in the design of a product, there is a tremendous opportunity to create products that will be successful and profitable.

There is a natural tendency for design, procurement, and manufacturing people to have different agendas unless their actions are coordinated. Design people are concerned with meeting the customer requirements. Procurement people are interested in getting the best prices from a group of pre-screened preferred suppliers. Folks in manufacturing are looking for simple fabrication and assembly methods and long production runs.

Cross functional product design teams with representatives from these three groups have the opportunity to blend the best insights from each group. Cross functional teams can review the new product design and discuss the relevant issues. Can existing preferred suppliers provide the components needed? How many new suppliers are needed? What opportunities are there to simplify the design and reduce the number of suppliers? What happens if a supplier stops producing a certain component? How can the assembly of the product be made easier?

At the same time they are reviewing product designs, a cross functional team can evaluate existing preferred suppliers and manufacturing
facilities. What components can existing suppliers provide? What are
their service levels and technical support capabilities? How large a
workforce and what kind of skills are needed to make the product?
How much capacity is needed and which facilities should be used?

A product design that does a good job of coordinating the three
perspectives—design, procurement, and manufacturing—will result in a
product that can be supported by an efficient supply chain. This will
give the product a fast time to market and a competitive cost.

Production Scheduling (Make)

Production scheduling allocates available capacity (equipment, labor,
and facilities) to the work that needs to be done. The goal is to use available capacity in the most efficient and profitable manner. The production scheduling operation is a process of finding the right balance
between several competing objectives:

- *High utilization rates*—This often means long production runs
  and centralized manufacturing and distribution centers. The
  idea is to generate and benefit from economies of scale.

- *Low inventory levels*—This usually means short production
  runs and just-in-time delivery of raw materials. The idea is to
  minimize the assets and cash tied up in inventory.

- *High levels of customer service*—Often requires high levels of
  inventory or many short production runs. The aim is to provide the customer with quick delivery of products and not to
  run out of stock in any product.

When a single product is to be made in a dedicated facility, scheduling means organizing operations as efficiently as possible and running
the facility at the level required to meet demand for the product. When

several different products are to be made in a single facility or on a single assembly line, this is more complex. Each product will need to be produced for some period of time and then time will be needed to switch over to production of the next product.

The first step in scheduling a multi-product production facility is to determine the economic lot size for the production runs of each product. This is a calculation much like the EOQ (economic order quantity) calculation used in the inventory control process. The calculation of economic lot size involves balancing the production set up costs for a product with the cost of carrying that product in inventory. If set ups are done frequently and production runs are done in small batches, the result will be low levels of inventory but the production costs will be higher due to increased set up activity. If production costs are minimized by doing long production runs, then inventory levels will be higher and product inventory carrying costs will be higher.

Once production quantities have been determined, the second step is to set the right sequence of production runs for each product. The basic rule is that if inventory for a certain product is low relative to its expected demand, then production of this product should be scheduled ahead of other products that have higher levels of inventory relative to their expected demand. A common technique is to schedule production runs based on the concept of a product's "run out time." The run out time is the number of days or weeks it would take to deplete the product inventory on hand given its expected demand. The run out time calculation for a product is expressed as

$$R = P / D$$

where

R = run out time

P = number of units of product on hand

D = product demand in units for a day or week

The scheduling process is a repetitive process that begins with a calculation of the run out times for all products—their R values. The first production run is then scheduled for the product with the lowest R value. Assume that the economic lot size for that product has been produced and then recalculate all product R values. Again, select the product with the lowest R value, and schedule its production run next. Assume the economic lot size is produced for this product and again recalculate

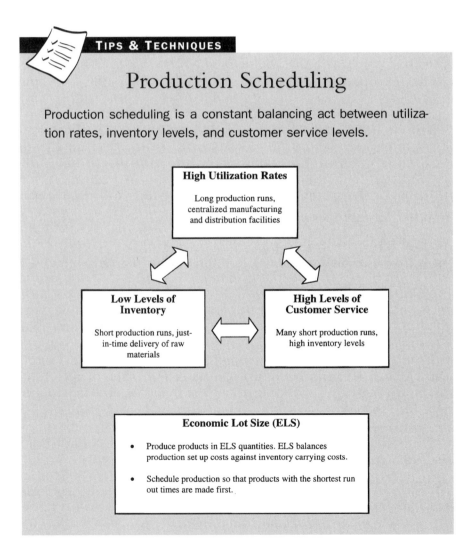

TIPS & TECHNIQUES

Production Scheduling

Production scheduling is a constant balancing act between utilization rates, inventory levels, and customer service levels.

High Utilization Rates

Long production runs, centralized manufacturing and distribution facilities

Low Levels of Inventory

Short production runs, just-in-time delivery of raw materials

High Levels of Customer Service

Many short production runs, high inventory levels

Economic Lot Size (ELS)

- Produce products in ELS quantities. ELS balances production set up costs against inventory carrying costs.

- Schedule production so that products with the shortest run out times are made first.

all product R values. This scheduling process can be repeated as often as necessary to create a production schedule going as far into the future as needed.

After scheduling is done, the resulting inventory should be continuously checked against actual demand. Is inventory building up too fast? Should the demand number be changed in the calculation of run out time? Reality rarely happens as planned so production schedules need to be constantly adjusted.

Facility Management (Make)

All facility management decisions happen within the constraints set by decisions about facility locations. Location is one of the five supply chain drivers discussed in Chapter 1. It is usually quite expensive to shut down a facility or to build a new one so companies live with the consequences of decisions they make about where to locate their facilities. Ongoing facility management takes location as a given and focuses on how best to use the capacity available. This involves making decisions in three areas:

1. The role each facility will play

2. How capacity is allocated in each facility

3. The allocation of suppliers and markets to each facility

The role each facility will play involves decisions that determine what activities will be performed in which facilities. These decisions have a big impact on the flexibility of the supply chain. They largely define the ways that the supply chain can change its operations to meet changing market demand. If a facility is designated to perform only a single function or serve only a single market, it usually cannot easily be shifted to perform a different function or serve a different market if supply chain needs change.

How capacity is allocated in each facility is dictated by the role that the facility plays. Capacity allocation decisions result in the equipment and labor that is employed at the facility. It is easier to change capacity allocation decisions than to change location decisions but still it is not cost effective to make frequent changes in allocation. So, once decided, capacity allocation strongly influences supply chain performance and profitability. Allocating too little capacity to a facility creates inability to meet demand and loss of sales. Too much capacity in a facility results in low utilization rates and higher supply chain costs.

The allocation of suppliers and markets to each facility is influenced by the first two decisions. Depending on the role that a facility plays and the capacity allocated to it, the facility will require certain kinds of suppliers and the products and volumes that it can handle mean that it can support certain types of markets. Decisions about the suppliers and markets to allocate to a facility will affect the costs for transporting supplies to the facility and transporting finished products from the facility to customers. These decisions also affect the overall supply chain's ability to meet market demands.

Order Management (Deliver)

Order management is the process of passing order information from customers back through the supply chain from retailers to distributors to service providers and producers. This process also includes passing information about order delivery dates, product substitutions, and back orders forward through the supply chain to customers. This process has long relied on the use of the telephone and paper documents such as purchase orders, sales orders, change orders, pick tickets, packing lists, and invoices.

A company generates a purchase order and calls a supplier to fill the order. The supplier who gets the call either fills the order from its own

IN THE REAL WORLD

Perkins (www.perkins1.com) is a distributor of food-service paper products, specialty and bakery foods, restaurant equipment, and sanitary supplies serving New England and the Mid-Atlantic states. The company has just completed a $2\frac{1}{2}$ year process of planning, building, and moving into their new headquarters and distribution center.

As the company grew and acquired other companies, it wound up operating out of six different locations. Over time it became increasingly apparent that this collection of facilities was not able to effectively support the business. Gary Perkins is the President and CEO while Larry Perkins is the company's Chief Operating Officer (COO). Larry offered, "We had duplicate inventory in these locations and we had five trucks and five drivers whose sole activity was moving inventory around between these locations. We were becoming less profitable in terms of return on sales even though total revenues continued to go up.

"Growth of SKUs created bottlenecks in the warehouse at the storage and picking slots and at the loading docks. Introduction of new product categories was stymied. And when we acquired companies there was no opportunity to fold their operations into our existing facilities. This caused us to squander efficiency realization."

People from the company traveled and visited other best-in-class facilities to see what other companies were doing. They also hired a consulting firm that specializes in facilities planning and design to work with them on the design of their new location. There were three main steps in the process. The first step was to figure, based on inventory requirements, the size of the new facility they needed. The second step was to choose the location for the facility and the last step was to design the operating procedures and systems and the building itself.

IN THE REAL WORLD (CONTINUED)

They analyzed the business and created projections for the growth of sales in each of their product categories. Design of the new building was based on six-year projections. "This means one year to build the building and five years of growth after that," said Larry. "We can go from a total of around 348,000 square feet now to 530,000 square feet in the future. We looked for property that would accommodate this size of a facility as well as provide us with space to expand later. We found the perfect location logistically but could not find the right land—so we kept looking in concentric circles out from there until we found a property that fit our needs, our personnel's needs, and our budget.

"Then we needed to decide what kind of warehouse operating procedures and systems to use. Different kinds of inventory and different product categories had different needs. In effect, what we did was to wrap the new buiilding around the inventory. We designed five kinds of aisles—conventional aisles, very narrow aisles, two kinds of high velocity storage aisles with a pick tunnel, and carousels. Each aisle has its own types of pallet positions and picking slots. The high velocity pick aisles accommodate our fastest turning items. The conventional aisles are for the items that are picked over 10 times per week and the very narrow aisles are for items we pick 10 or less times a week. The carousels handle small box items or broken cases."

The new facility was also designed to accommodate other needs. There are very deep loading docks to allow fast loading and unloading of trucks. The loading docks also accommodate cross docking. There are parts of the warehouse with different temperatures—ambient room temperature, frozen temperature, and also a cool termperature area to support new product lines.

A lot of thought went into the design of the administrative and training areas of the facility and into an area to showcase equipment and supplies that the company sells. "We actually built these areas to accommodate 10-year projections," said Larry. "We have a much larger auditorium for group meetings and presentations. And we added a test kitchen to support in-house meals and "cuttings" of foods being considered for stocking. The test kitchen also showcases our restaurant equipment offerings. The site layout, technical capabilities, size, and design features make this one of the best foodservice distribution facilities in the country."

As they began to move into the new facility, timing and coordination were critical. "We moved our smaller locations into the building first. It gave us time to try out new procedures and debug them. We use RF (radio frequency) and bar coding for receiving, drops, picking, and inventory control. We use picking techniques like route picking and wave picking. We needed to train our people, try out the technology, and make adjustments without disrupting our ongoing business."

The cost of building the new facility will be paid for by increased operating efficiencies in the next two to three years. Efficiencies will also be gained in reduced rent and utilities costs, lower inventory carrying costs, and reduced operating expenses. Larry pointed out some other significant benefits, "All my competitors have the same products that I do so I need to offer other capabilities to attract customers. Now we can provide increased customer service levels and a range of other offerings to customers. This facility is also very beneficial in helping us to attract and retain good people. People like to be associated with success."

As a company enters into a new phase of its growth, having the right facilities to support that growth are key to its continued success. Larry Perkins summed up the company's move by saying, "Our management team the last few years has been buried by the day-to-day demands of just running the business because of the complexity of it all. Now with this move we can get back to focusing on how to make the business more efficient and looking into the more long term growth and profit issues."

inventory or sources required products from other suppliers. If the supplier fills the order from its inventory, it turns the customer purchase order into a pick ticket, a packing list, and an invoice. If products are sourced from other suppliers, the original customer purchase order is turned into a purchase order from the first supplier to the next supplier. That supplier in turn will either fill the order from its inventory or source products from other suppliers. The purchase order it receives is again turned into documents such as pick tickets, packing lists, and invoices. This process is repeated through the length of the supply chain.

In the last 20 years or so, supply chains have become noticeably more complex than they previously were. Companies now deal with multiple tiers of suppliers, outsourced service providers, and distribution channel partners. This complexity has evolved in response to changes in the way products are sold, increased customer service expectations, and the need to respond quickly to new market demands.

The traditional order management process has longer lead and lag times built into it due to the slow movement of data back and forth in the supply chain. This slow movement of data works well enough in some simple supply chains, but in complex supply chains faster and more accurate movement of data is necessary to achieve the responsiveness and efficiency that is needed. Modern order management focuses on techniques to enable faster and more accurate movement of order related data.

In addition, the order management process needs to do exception handling and provide people with ways to quickly spot problems and give them the information they need to take corrective action. This means the processing of routine orders should be automated and orders that require special handling because of issues such as insufficient inventory, missed delivery dates, or customer change requests need to be brought to the attention of people who can handle these issues.

Because of these requirements, order management is beginning to overlap and merge with a function called customer relationship management (CRM) that is often thought of as a marketing and sales function.

Because of supply chain complexity and changing market demands, order management is a process that is evolving rapidly. However, a handful of basic principles can be listed that guide this operation:

- *Enter the order data once and only once*—Capture the data electronically as close to its original source as possible and do not manually reenter the data as it moves through the supply chain. It is usually best if the customers themselves enter their orders into an order entry system. This system should then transfer the relevant order data to other systems and supply chain participants as needed for creation of purchase orders, pick tickets, invoices, and so on.

- *Automate the order handling*—Manual intervention should be minimized for the routing and filling of routine orders. Computer systems should send needed data to the appropriate locations to fulfill routine orders. Exception handling should identify orders with problems that require people to get involved to fix them.

- *Make order status visible to customers and service agents*—Let customers track their orders through all the stages from entry of the order to delivery of the products. Customers should be able to see order status on demand without having to enlist the assistance of other people. When an order runs into problems, bring the order to the attention of service agents who can resolve the problems.

- *Integrate order management systems with other related systems to maintain data integrity*—Order entry systems need product descriptive data and product prices to guide the customer in making their choices. The systems that maintain this product data should communicate with order management systems.

Order data is needed by other systems to update inventory status, calculate delivery schedules, and generate invoices. Order data should automatically flow into these systems in an accurate and timely manner.

TIPS & TECHNIQUES

Four Rules for
Efficient Order Management

1. Enter the Order Once and Only Once

Capture the order electronically as close to the original source as possible. Do not manually reenter the order.

2. Automate Order Routing

Automatically send orders to appropriate fulfillment locations. People do only exception handling.

3. Make Order Status Visible

Let customers and service agents see order status information automatically whenever they want.

4. Use Integrated Order Management Systems

Electronically connect order management systems with other related systems to maintain data integrity.

Delivery Scheduling (Deliver)

The delivery scheduling operation is of course strongly affected by the decisions made concerning the modes of transportation that will be used. The delivery scheduling process works within the constraints set by transportation decisions. For most modes of transportation there are two types of delivery methods: direct deliveries and milk run deliveries.

Direct Deliveries

Direct deliveries are deliveries made from one originating location to one receiving location. With this method of delivery the routing is simply a matter of selecting the shortest path between the two locations. Scheduling this type of delivery involves decisions about the quantity to deliver and the frequency of deliveries to each location. The advantages of this delivery method are found in the simplicity of operations and delivery coordination. Since this method moves products directly from the location where they are made or stored in inventory to a location where the products will be used, it eliminates any intermediate operations that combine different smaller shipments into a single, combined larger shipment.

Direct deliveries are efficient if the receiving location generates economic order quantities (EOQs) that are the same size as the shipment quantities needed to make best use of the transportation mode being used. For instance, if a receiving location gets deliveries by truck and its EOQ is the same size as a truck load (TL) then the direct delivery method makes sense. If the EOQ does not equal TL quantities, then this delivery method becomes less efficient. Receiving expenses incurred at the receiving location are high because this location must handle separate deliveries from the different suppliers of all the products it needs.

Milk Run Deliveries

Milk run deliveries are deliveries that are routed to either bring products from a single originating location to multiple receiving locations or deliveries that bring products from multiple originating locations to a single receiving location. Scheduling milk run deliveries is a much more complex task than scheduling direct deliveries. Decisions must be made about delivery quantities of different products, about the frequency of deliveries, and most importantly about the routing and sequencing of pickups and deliveries.

The advantages of this method of delivery are in the fact that more efficient use can be made of the mode of transportation used and the cost of receiving deliveries is lower because receiving locations get fewer and larger deliveries. If the EOQs of different products needed by a receiving location are less than truck load (LTL) amounts, milk run deliveries allow orders for different products to be combined until the resulting quantity equals a truck load or TL amount. If there are many receiving locations that each need smaller amounts of products, they can all be served by a single truck that starts its delivery route with a TL amount of products.

There are two main techniques for routing milk run deliveries. Each routing technique has its strengths and weaknesses and each technique is more or less effective depending on the situation in which it is used and the accuracy of the data that is available. Both of these techniques are supported by software packages. The two techniques are:

- The savings matrix technique
- The generalized assignment technique

The savings matrix technique is the simpler of the two techniques and can be used to assign customers to vehicles and to design routes where there are delivery time windows at receiving locations and other constraints. The technique is robust and can be modified to take into account many different constraints. It provides a reasonably good routing solution that can be put to practical use. Its weakness lies in the fact that it is often possible to find more cost effective solutions using the generalized assignment technique. This technique is best used when there are many different constraints that need to be satisfied by the delivery schedule.

The generalized assignment technique is more sophisticated and usually gives a better solution than the savings matrix technique when there are no constraints on the delivery schedule other than the carrying capacity of the delivery vehicle. The disadvantage of this technique is that it has a harder time generating good delivery schedules as more and more constraints are included. This technique is best used when the delivery constraints are limited to vehicle capacity or to total travel time.

Delivery Sources

Deliveries can be made to customers from two sources:

- Single product locations
- Distribution centers

Single product locations are facilities such as factories or warehouses where a single product or a narrow range of related items are available for shipment. These facilities are appropriate when there is a predictable and high level of demand for the products they offer and where shipments will be made only to customer locations that can receive the products in large, bulk amounts. They offer great economies of scale when used effectively.

Distribution centers are facilities where bulk shipments of products arrive from single product locations. When suppliers are located a long distance away from customers, the use of a distribution center provides for economies of scale in long-distance transportation to bring large amounts of products to a location close to the final customers.

The distribution center may warehouse inventory for future shipment or it may be used primarily for crossdocking. Crossdocking is a technique pioneered by Wal-Mart where truckload shipments of single products arrive and are unloaded. At the same time these trucks are being unloaded, their bulk shipments are being broken down into smaller lots and combined with small lots of other products and loaded right back onto other trucks. These trucks then deliver the products to their final locations.

Distribution centers that use crossdocking provide several benefits. The first is that product flows faster in the supply chain since little inventory is held in storage. The second is that there is less handling expense since product does not have to be put away and then retrieved later from storage. The benefits of crossdocking can be realized when there are large predictable product volumes and when economies of scale can be had on both the inbound and outbound transportation. However, crossdocking is a demanding technique and it requires a considerable degree of coordination between inbound and outbound shipments.

Transporting and delivering goods is expensive so capabilities in this area are closely aligned with the actual needs of the market that the supply chain serves. Highly responsive supply chains usually have high transport and delivery costs because their customers expect quick delivery. This results in many small shipments of product. Less responsive supply chains can aggregate orders over a period of time and make fewer and larger shipments. This results in more economies of scale and lower transport costs.

Eastern Bag & Paper Company (www.eastern-bag.com) is a distributor of paper products, industrial packaging, foodservice, and janitorial and sanitary maintenance products. It operates out of two distribution centers, one in Connecticut and one in Massachusetts and has a fleet of 44 straight trucks and 4 tractor trailers. More than four million cases are shipped and 200,000 deliveries are made each year.

Eastern Bag & Paper has developed a very efficient delivery scheduling operation and it continues to innovate and refine the processes that support this operation. Meredith Reuben is the company's CEO and Don Burton is the Director of Operations. "Don has put a process in place," said Meredith Reuben, "and he continuously measures and refines the process so that it supports high levels of customer service and is at the same time very cost efficient. He has saved the company a lot of money."

The process begins at 4:00 p.m. every business day. All orders received up to that time are downloaded from the ERP (enterprise resource planning) system to an automatic delivery routing system called RoadShow. "We have built in customized parameters," Don explained. "Things like tight delivery windows for certain customers and route preferences so the system creates routes and schedules that are very efficient." It takes the RoadShow system and our router about two hours to calculate the routes and schedules for all the trucks.

At 6:00 p.m. the routes and schedules are uploaded back into the ERP and the picking labels are printed in each of the distribution centers. By 6:30 p.m. each location has a complete set of pick labels. The pick labels at each location are tailored to the way each warehouse is laid out. The pick labels tell the picker where to go for each item and what quantity to retrieve. Along with the labels that are attached to each case, a pick list is generated to accommodate a quality control audit.

"We have a QA process that randomly selects orders to audit," Don said. "We use the pick list and check it against the set of labels on each case. We probably audit about 10 percent of orders. We track errors such as "right label on wrong case," or "short, case not on truck," or "short, can't find case." Errors are traced back to the individuals who caused them and we show these people what they did wrong."

Loading the trucks takes 8 to 10 hours. Loading starts by 7:00 p.m. and is usually finished by 4:00 a.m. The trucks are on the road soon after. All trucks are equipped with a GPS (global positioning satellite) system. This system can pinpoint the location of each truck during the day and it creates an activity log that records the truck's movements.

"RoadShow creates a delivery schedule and GPS allows us to compare the actual route versus the planned route," Don explained. "The drivers are always saying RoadShow doesn't accurately reflect conditions. We can now create very realistic RoadShow schedules using corrective information that we get from GPS. Drivers are able to achieve 95 percent on-time performance against the schedules that we create."

The company continuously measures their performance and makes adjustments as needed to maintain high levels of customer service. There is a zero defect program in place which follows a customer order from entry to delivery. Meredith explained that, "We track 'perfect orders' and rate ourselves on that. A perfect order is an order that results in a perfect delivery—the complete order delivered to the right place at the right time, and a perfect invoice—all items correctly priced and identified. Most companies only track order fill rates. We take a more inclusive view of order fulfillment by using the perfect order concept. When we first started tracking we were only around 53 percent perfect. We are now in the low 80s and will soon hit 85 percent perfect."

"Our performance measurements allow us to track individual productivity and error rates by worker," said Don. "We have developed standard productivity rates for different jobs that we can use to compare against the actual productivity of each person. Our error reports allow us to identify the person and the department where an error originated. This is the information we need to continuously make adjustments to our operations so as to keep up high service levels and also keep our costs as low as possible."

It is the continuous measuring and adjusting that makes the activities of delivery scheduling and order fulfillment into a core competency. For the vast majority of distributors, regardless of the products they distribute, these two activities must be core competencies if the company is to be successful. "Bottom line, distribution is a 2 percent to 4 percent net business and there is no room for errors and low productivity," Meredith observed. "Measuring people and processes to look for improvements is something that goes on all the time. Process reengineering and investments in new technology to decrease errors and increase productivity is something that we do every year."

Supply Chain Operations Can Be Outsourced

After reading about the 10 basic supply chain operations in this chapter and the previous one, which of these operations are done by in-house staff in your company? How many of these operations are core competencies? How many of these operations bring money into your company and how many of them consume money?

The relentless pressure on profit margins that free markets create is a driving force behind the growth of outsourcing. What may be considered as overhead for Company A may be a service that Company B can offer and make a profit doing so. Company B may be able to offer this service for a price lower than it costs Company A to do it in-house. Company A is going to consider outsourcing.

The traditional participants in supply chains are producers, logistics providers, distributors, and retailers. How many of the 10 supply chain operations can be called core competencies of any of these organizations? There are some operations such as credit and collections, product design, and order management that may not be a core competency of any of the traditional participants. This creates opportunities for new service providers to take on these operations and offer them to the other supply chain participants. All 10 of these operations need to be done for the supply chain as a whole, but they do not all need to be done by any single company and indeed they cannot all be done well by any single company.

The other force that drives outsourcing is the growing sophistication of the markets that supply chains serve. Gone are the days when Ford Motor Company could run a vertically integrated company that did everything from mine iron ore to produce steel to design and build automobiles. That structure was only possible because the markets it served were content to buy mass quantities of standard products. As Henry Ford said when asked about what colors his customers could choose from, "They can have any color they want as long as it's black." Markets today demand and pay for all sorts of innovations, customized features, and services. This creates complexity in the supply chain and participants who specialize in certain areas bring the expertise and efficiencies that are required to manage this complexity.

Many of the supply chain management concepts originated in the manufacturing sector. Professor Wallace Hopp is the Breed University Professor and a director of the Master of Management and Manufacturing Program at the McCormick School of Engineering and Kellogg Graduate School of Management, Northwestern University. He is co-author of *Factory Physics*.

Historically, many of the trends and techniques that now guide supply chain management originated in the manufacturing sector. Professor Hopp points out one such technique that now gets a lot of attention in supply chain management. It is a technique called variability pooling or postponement. "Using this technique manufacturers and now whole supply chains can make and stock inventory composed of generic parts and then assemble these parts only at the last moment to create a specific final product." Manufacturers such as Hewlett Packard developed this technique because it allowed them to build and keep on hand large inventories of parts from which to quickly assemble finished goods. At the same time they were able to defer much of the risk of holding that inventory.

A lot of the risk of holding inventory comes from the chance that it will not match market demand and become obsolete. "If a company or supply chain keeps its inventory as parts that can be assembled into a number of different final products, then there is the opportunity to quickly build a final product only when the demand for that specific product exists. The risk of building any product beforehand based on imperfect demand forecasts is avoided."

In order for companies in a supply chain to employ this technique, it creates a need for these companies to collaborate in the design process. And collaborative design is a growing trend in many supply chains. This is especially apparent in the supply chains that feed the automotive industry. "The big car companies are looking for ways to get their suppliers more involved in the design of new vehicles. They are driving the design function down not just to their tier one suppliers but even further down to the suppliers of those suppliers." The idea is to design a car composed of many generic modules. "This can really shorten the time to market for a new product. Honda is getting very good at this so they get new cars to market faster than other car makers. They do this by breaking a new car into sub-sections that can be designed and built simultaneously by different suppliers and then delivered to Honda for final assembly."

When asked about the trend away from vertical integration toward outsourcing, Professor Hopp feels that there are limits to how far outsourcing can go and that some companies are now bumping up against those limits. For instance he said, "Ford has worked with some of its suppliers to create the Ford suppliers industrial park, south of Chicago, next to its factory that is gearing up to produce its crossover vehicle. Co-located suppliers have built their plants right next to the Ford plant. The advantages are that engineers can talk with each other and the movement of parts from one plant to another is very quick. The disadvantages are that this arrangement is very much like having one vertically integrated operation. Since everyone is in the same location, problems that affect one company will probably also affect the others such as labor unrest, transportation delays, or power outages.

"Some companies have swung back a bit on outsourcing and brought operations back in house. If you are a big enough company why wouldn't you do as much of the common commodity manufacturing as you can? You get economies of scale when you do this. The more different products that you make, the more products that you can make a profit margin on. If all you are actually making is 5 percent of your final product then you don't have much to defend or work with. You are in danger of defining yourself so narrowly that you lose the ability to spot new trends and new applications for your products.

"A company has to be very careful, however, to select what it can compete on. It has to know what its core competencies are. Breed Technologies is a well-known maker of automotive safety systems. For a while they were very successful in making a lot of generic parts that were later assembled into finished products. In the end though, the products they were making got outside of their core competencies and they ran into trouble."

Chapter Summary

The Make category includes the operations required to develop and build the products and services that a supply chain provides. Operations that are in this category are: product design; production management; and facility and management. The Deliver category of operations encompasses the activities that are part of receiving customer orders and delivering products to customers. The two main operations are order entry/order fulfillment and product delivery. These two operations constitute the core connections between companies in a supply chain.

The relentless pressure on profit margins that free markets create is a driving force behind the growth of outsourcing. What may be considered as overhead for Company A may be a service that Company B can offer and make a profit doing so. Company B may be able to offer this service for a price lower than it costs Company A to do it in-house. Company A is going to consider outsourcing.

CHAPTER 4

Supply Chain Coordination and Use of Technology

After reading this chapter you will be able to

- Understand a common supply chain dynamic that is a major contributor to the "boom to bust" business cycle

- Appreciate the factors that contribute to this supply chain dynamic

- Evaluate ways to combat this dynamic

- Assess the technology that is available to support and enable effective supply chain coordination

The spread of high speed data communications networks and computer technology has made it possible to manage the supply chain with a level of precision that was not feasible as recently as the mid-1980s. Those organizations that learn to use the techniques and technologies that are now available can build supply chains that have a competitive advantage in their markets.

Because the capability exists to react much more quickly to changes in market demand, this capability is now a point of competition. Business competition based on supply chain efficiency is becoming a central fact in many markets. To develop this capability, individual companies and entire supply chains need to learn new behaviors and they need to enable these new behaviors with the use of appropriate technology.

The "Bullwhip" Effect

One of the most common dynamics in supply chains is a phenomena that has been dubbed "the bullwhip effect." What happens is that small changes in product demand by the consumer at the front of the supply chain translate into wider and wider swings in demand experienced by companies further back in the supply chain. Companies at different stages in the supply chain come to have very different pictures of market demand and the result is a breakdown in supply chain coordination. Companies behave in ways that at first create product shortages and then lead to an excess supply of products.

This dynamic plays out on a larger scale in certain industries in what is called a "boom to bust" business cycle. In particular this affects industries that serve developing and growth markets where demand can suddenly grow. Good examples of this can be found in the industries that serve the telecommunications equipment or computer components markets. The cycle starts when strong market demand creates a shortage of product. Distributors and manufacturers steadily increase their inventories and production rates in response to the demand. At some point either demand changes or the supply of product exceeds the demand level. Distributors and manufacturers do not at first realize that supply exceeds demand and they continue building the supply. Finally the glut of product is so large that everyone realizes there is too much. Manufacturers shut down plants and lay off workers. Distributors are stuck with inventories that decrease in value and can take years to work down.

This dynamic can be modeled in a simple supply chain that contains a retailer, a distributor, and a manufacturer. In the 1960s a simulation game was developed by the Massachusetts Institute of Technology's Sloan School of Management that illustrates how the bullwhip effect develops. The simulation game they developed is called the "beer game." It shows what happens in a hypothetical supply chain that supports a group of retail stores that sell beer, snacks, and other convenience items. The results of the beer game simulation teach a lot about how to coordinate the actions of different companies in a supply chain.

Peter Senge in his book, *The Fifth Discipline* (Senge, Peter M., 1990, *The Fifth Discipline: The Art and Practice of the Learning Organization,* New York: Doubleday/Currency, Chapter 3), devotes a chapter to exploring how the bullwhip effect gathers momentum and what can be done to avoid it. The beer game starts with retailers experiencing a sudden but small increase in customer demand for a certain brand of beer called Lover's Beer. Orders are batched up by retailers and passed on to the distributors who deliver the beer. Initially, these orders exceed the inventory that distributors have on hand so they ration out their supplies of Lover's Beer to the retailers and place even larger orders for the beer with the brewery that makes Lover's Beer. The brewery cannot instantly increase production of the beer so it rations out the beer it can produce to the distributors and begins building additional production capacity.

At first the scarcity of the beer prompts panic buying and hoarding behavior. Then as the brewery ramps up its production rate and begins shipping the product in large quantities, the orders that had been steadily increasing due to panic buying suddenly decline. The glut of product fills up the distributors' warehouses, fills all the retailers' unfilled back orders, and exceeds the actual consumer demand. The brewery is left with excess production capacity, the distributors are stuck with excess inventory, and the retailers either cancel their beer orders or run discount promotions to move the product. Everybody loses money. Exhibit 4.1 illustrates how each company sees product demand and the distortion that causes such havoc.

The costs of the bullwhip effect are felt by all members of the supply chain. Manufacturers add extra production capacity to satisfy an order stream that is much more volatile than actual demand. Distributors carry

EXHIBIT 4.1

Product Demand Distortion Swings (The "Bullwhip" Effect)

Inventory levels in supply chain over time illustrating the wild swings that develop as product demand distortion moves from customer to retailer to distributor to manufacturer. Swings in product demand appear more pronounced to companies further up the supply chain. This distortion makes effective supply chain management very difficult.

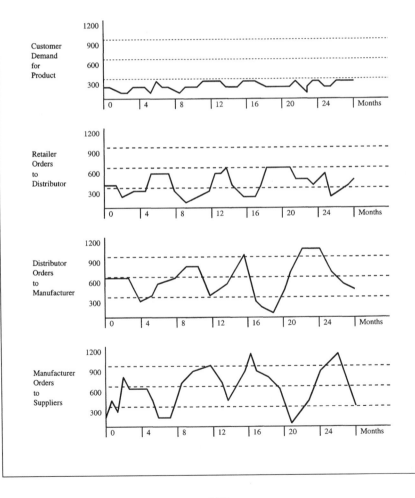

extra inventory to cover the variability in order levels. Transportation costs increase because excess transportation capacity has to be added to cover the periods of high demand. Along with transportation costs, labor costs also go up in order to respond to the high demand periods. Retailers experience problems with product availability and extended replenishment lead times. During periods of high demand, there are times when the available capacity and inventory in the supply chain cannot cover the orders being placed. This results in product rationing, longer order replenishment cycles, and lost sales due to lack of inventory.

Coordination in the Supply Chain

Research into the bullwhip effect has identified five major factors that cause the effect. These factors interact with each other in different combinations in different supply chains but the net effect is that they generate the wild demand swings that make it so hard to run an efficient supply chain. These factors must be understood and addressed in order to coordinate the actions of any supply chain. They are:

1. Demand forecasting
2. Order batching
3. Product rationing
4. Product pricing
5. Performance incentives

Demand Forecasting

Demand forecasting based on orders received instead of end user demand data will inherently become more and more inaccurate as it moves up the supply chain. Companies that are removed from contact with the end user can lose touch with actual market demand if they view their role as simply filling the orders placed with them by their immediate customers. Each company in a supply chain sees fluctuations in the orders that come to them that are caused by the bullwhip effect. When they use this order data to do their demand forecasts, they just add further distortion to the demand picture and pass this distortion along in the form of orders that they place with their suppliers.

Clearly, one way to counteract this distortion in demand forecasts is for all companies in a supply chain to share a common set of demand data from which to do their forecasting. The most accurate source of this demand data is the supply chain member closest to the end use customer (if not the end use customers themselves). Sharing point-of-sales (POS) data among all the companies in a supply chain goes a long way toward taming the bullwhip effect because it lets everyone respond to actual market demand instead of supply chain distortions.

Order Batching

Order batching occurs because companies place orders periodically for amounts of product that will minimize their order processing and transportation costs. As discussed in the section on inventory control in Chapter 2, companies tend to order in lot sizes determined by the EOQ (economic order quantity). Because of order batching, these orders vary from the level of actual demand and this variance is magnified as it moves up the supply chain.

The way to address demand distortion caused by order batching is to find ways to reduce the cost of order processing and transportation. This will cause EOQ lot sizes to get smaller and orders to be placed more frequently. The result will be a smoother flow of orders that distributors and manufacturers will be able to handle more efficiently. Ordering costs can be reduced by using electronic ordering technology. Transportation costs can be reduced by using third party logistics suppliers (3PLs) to cost effectively pick up many small shipments from suppliers and deliver small orders to many customers.

Product Rationing

This is the response that manufacturers take when they are faced with more demand than they can meet. One common rationing approach is for a manufacturer to allocate the available supply of product based on the number of orders received. Thus if the available supply equals 70 percent of the orders received, the manufacturer will fill 70 percent of the amount of each order and back order the rest. This leads distributors and retailers in the supply chain to raise their order quantities artificially in order to increase the amount of product that gets rationed to them. This behavior greatly overstates product demand and it is called "shortage gaming."

There are several ways to respond to this. Manufacturers can base their rationing decisions on the historical ordering patterns of a given distributor or retailer and not on their present order sizes. This eliminates much of the motivation for the shortage gaming that otherwise occurs. Manufacturers and distributors can also alert their customers in advance if they see demand outstripping supply. This way product shortages will not take buyers by surprise and there will be less panic buying.

Product Pricing

Product pricing causes product prices to fluctuate, resulting in distortions of product demand. If special sales are offered and product prices are lowered, it will induce customers to buy more product or to buy product sooner than they otherwise would (forward buying). Then prices return to normal levels and demand falls off. Instead of a smooth flow of products through the supply chain, price fluctuations can create waves of demand and surges of product flow that are hard to handle efficiently.

Answers to this problem generally revolve around the concept of "everyday low prices." If the end customers for a product believe that they will get a good price whenever they purchase the product, they will make purchases based on real need and not other considerations. This in turn makes demand easier to forecast and companies in the supply chain can respond more efficiently.

Performance Incentives

These are often different for different companies and individuals in a supply chain. Each company can see its job as managing its position in isolation from the rest of the supply chain. Within companies, individuals can also see their job in isolation from the rest of the company. It is common for companies to structure incentives that reward a company's sales force on sales made each month or each quarter. Therefore as the end of a month or a quarter approaches, the sales force offers discounts and takes other measures to move product in order to meet quotas. This results in product for which there is no real demand being pushed into the supply chain. It is also common for managers within a company to be motivated by incentives that conflict with other company objectives. For instance, a transportation manager may take actions that minimize transportation costs at the expense of customer service or inventory carrying costs.

Alignment of performance incentives with supply chain efficiencies is a real challenge. It begins with the use of accurate activity based costing (ABC) data that can highlight the associated costs. Companies need to quantify the expenses incurred by forward buying due to month-end or end-of-quarter sales incentives. Companies also need to identify the effect of conflicting internal performance incentives. The next step is to experiment with new incentive plans that support efficient supply chain operation. This is a process that each company needs to work through in its own way.

Eliyahu Goldratt wrote a book titled, *The Goal*, about a factory manager's quest to save his factory from being closed down for lack of profitability. It chronicles the process that the manager and his staff go through as they learn how to save their factory. What they learn is how to apply the principles of what Mr. Goldratt calls the "Theory of Constraints."

Mr. Goldratt and others have realized that the theory of constraints applies equally well to the operation of a whole supply chain as to the operation of a single factory within a supply chain. Lawrence Fredendall and Ed Hill in their book, *Basics of Supply Chain Management* (Fredendall, Lawrence D., and Ed Hill, 2001, *Basics of Supply Chain Management*, Boca Raton, FL: St. Lucie Press), have put forth a clear explanation for how to apply the theory of constraints to synchronize the operations of a supply chain.

The theory of constraints provides a useful model to conceptualize and manage the supply chain within a single company or across a collection of companies. The theory of constraints is based upon the idea that all systems have at least one constraint and that it is better to manage constraints than to try to eliminate them. This is because when one part of a system ceases to be a constraint, a different constraint will occur in another part of the system. This is inevitable because the capacities of each part of a system are not all the same. So instead of forever reacting to new constraints or bottlenecks as they appear, why not choose a small group of constraints and manage them deliberately and efficiently?

To apply this model, the first step is to define the goal and decide what measurements will be used to measure progress toward the goal. Mr. Goldratt's definition of the goal for a manufacturing company also works for a supply chain. The goal is defined as "Increase

throughput while simultaneously reducing both inventory and operating expense." Throughput is the rate at which sales to end customers occur.

Once a goal has been defined and there is agreement on how to
measure progress toward the goal, it is possible to apply the five
focusing steps. These steps help clarify the situation being investigated and lead to the decisions necessary to reach the goal. The five
steps are:

1 *Identify the system's bottlenecks or constraints*—Trace out
the workflows and the paths that materials travel in a factory or a
supply chain. Find out where slowdowns and backups occur.

2 *Decide how to exploit these bottlenecks*—Figure out how to
maximize the operation of those activities that are bottlenecks.
The rate of throughput for the entire system is set by the rate
of throughput achieved by the bottlenecks. Ensure the bottlenecks operate at maximum capacity by providing them with
enough inventory so that they can continue to operate even if
there are occasional slowdowns elsewhere in the system.

3 *Subordinate everything else to the above decision*—Do not
try to maximize the operation of a non-bottleneck operation.
Additional productivity achieved by non-bottleneck operations
that exceeds the capacity of the bottlenecks to process will be
neutralized anyway by the slowdowns and backups caused at
the bottlenecks. Synchronize all system operations to the rates
that can be efficiently processed by the bottleneck operations.

4 *Elevate the system's bottlenecks*—Add additional processing
capacity to the bottleneck activities. Since the rate of throughput
of the entire system is set by the throughput of the bottlenecks,
improvements in the bottlenecks will increase the efficiency of
the entire system and provide the best return on investment.

5 *If, in a previous step, a bottleneck has been broken, go back
to step 1*—As the capacity of one system bottleneck is elevated,
it may cease to be a bottleneck. The bottleneck may transfer to

another operation that could keep up before but now cannot keep up with the new increase in capacity. Watch the entire system to see where slowdowns and backups occur; they may shift from one area to another. If this occurs, start again at step 1.

The theory of constraints says that the throughput of the whole system is set by the capacity of the bottlenecks. Exhibit 4.2 shows a sample diagram of workflows and bottlenecks in a factory. This model of workflows in a factory can be applied to the workflows in a supply chain. One constraint or bottleneck in every supply chain is the demand that is generated by the market that the supply chain serves. In many cases, market demand is the only constraint because supply of products equals or exceeds demand. In cases where demand exceeds supply there will be some other constraints elsewhere in the supply chain. If we apply this model to a supply chain we get a powerful method to organize and manage supply chain operations.

EXHIBIT 4.2

Flow of Work and Inventory through a Factory

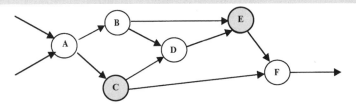

The bottlenecks or constraints in the flow of work through this factory are operations C and E. The productivity set by these two operations sets the pace for the ENTIRE factory. Productivity improvements in the other operations will not result in any improvement in the productivity of the factory as a whole. Apply the five focusing steps to manage this system and move it toward the goal defined for it.

A very effective response to the bullwhip effect is to manage the entire supply chain as a single entity and to synchronize it to the timing of actual market demand. Exhibit 4.3 illustrates this idea. This can happen if the supply chain participants closest to the end use customers share their sales numbers and their sales forecasts with the other companies in the supply chain. Each company can then manage their actions based on the most accurate data about market demand.

Buffers in the supply chain are determined by the degree of uncertainty about future market demand and the service levels required by the market. The lower the uncertainty about demand, the smaller the buffers can be and still maintain high service levels. Companies can manage their buffers by using either productive capacity or inventory, whichever is most cost effective for them.

Synchronized supply chains avoid the volatile waves of demand that are generated by the bullwhip effect. And increased predictability makes the productivity of each company easier to manage and the supply chain as a whole becomes more efficient and profitable.

EXHIBIT 4.3

Flow of Inventory through a Synchronized Supply Chain

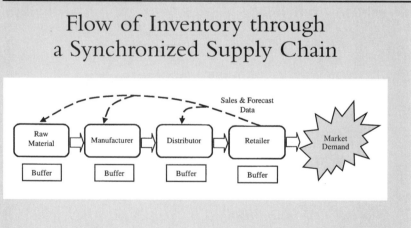

This model is called "drum-buffer-rope." Market demand is the constraint on the system and it sets the drum beat or pace of the supply chain. Individual companies manage uncertainty in their stage of the supply chain by using a buffer of either inventory or productive capacity. Buffers are kept low because uncertainty is minimized by sharing market demand data. This data is the rope that ties the participants together and allows them to synchronize their actions.

Collaborative Planning, Forecasting, and Replenishment

To facilitate the coordination that is needed in supply chains, an industry group known as the Voluntary Interindustry Commerce Standards (VICS) group has set up a committee to investigate collaborative planning, forecasting, and replenishment issues (CPFR). This committee documents best practices for CPFR and creates guidelines to follow for CPFR.

The CPFR process is divided into the three activities of planning, forecasting, and replenishment. Within each activity there are several steps:

Collaborative Planning

- Negotiate a front-end agreement that defines the responsibilities of the companies that will collaborate with each other

- Build a joint business plan that shows how the companies will work together to meet demand

Collaborative Forecasting

- Create sales forecasts for all the collaborating companies

- Identify any exceptions or differences between companies

- Resolve the exceptions to provide a common sales forecast

Collaborative Replenishment

- Create order forecasts for all the collaborating companies
- Identify exceptions between companies
- Resolve the exceptions to provide an efficient production and delivery schedule
- Generate actual orders to meet customer demand

CPFR in Action

For an example of how CPFR can work let's return to the example of Nimble Company. In the section on product design in Chapter 2, we saw how Nimble Company developed a home entertainment system that was much simpler to manufacture than a competitor's system. This simpler design is in turn supported by a less complex supply chain that reduces production costs and increases responsiveness to market demands. All of this is central to the competitive success that Nimble Co. is enjoying.

Nimble Co. has collaboration agreements in place with its supply chain partners and has an ongoing planning, forecasting, and replenishment process in place with these partners. Nimble Co. receives POS data that show the actual sales of its systems in retail stores. From these same retailers, Nimble Co. receives regular updates of their sales forecasts and their inventory levels of Nimble Co. home entertainment systems. Nimble Co. uses this data to plan its production schedule and it also shares this data with the component manufacturers who provide parts for its home entertainment system. This way the component manufacturers can plan their own production schedules.

In looking at the sales data and forecasts, Nimble Co. sees that demand for their product is growing faster than anticipated in their yearly plan and they need to increase production. Nimble Co. revises its production schedule for the year and takes the new plan to its key component suppliers to negotiate additional purchases of their components. It turns out that one component supplier cannot quickly ramp up their production but a second supplier has a component that could fill the need with just a slight modification to the design of one part of Nimble Co.'s home entertainment system. Because all affected parties know what is going on and have enough lead time, the design changes are made and production schedules are increased to meet the rise in product demand without any retailers running out of inventory.

The benefits illustrated in this scenario are numerous. To begin with, the bullwhip effect is diminished because all companies in the supply chain can see real time sales data and share sales forecasts. This allows everyone to optimize their production schedules, inventory levels, and delivery schedules. Next there are the benefits associated with Nimble Co. being able to quickly see a real rise in customer demand and coordinate with its suppliers to increase production schedules over previously planned levels. Even though one component supplier was not able to accommodate Nimble Co.'s increased production schedule, another supplier had a workable substitute. Changes were made to the product design, production was increased, and no retailer lost sales revenue due to running out of inventory.

Those companies that can create collaborative supply chains will have a significant competitive advantage. Collaboration is not easy to implement and it will take time to become more common in business. However, prominent companies are already beginning to lead the way. Companies such as Wal-Mart, Dell, and Proctor & Gamble share point of sales data with all the other companies in their respective supply chains. The companies in these supply chains are also starting to share inventory data with each other. Sharing this kind of information provides a basis for each company to make decisions about its own activities that will yield better efficiencies and profits for itself and for the supply chain as a whole.

How to Start Supply Chain Collaboration

The best place to start in any effort to promote collaboration is to measure the bullwhip effect within your company. Over a period of time such as a quarter or a year, compare the volume and frequency of orders you receive from your customers with the volume and frequency of orders you place with your suppliers. Plot them out on a graph so everyone can see the divergence between incoming customer orders and your outgoing supplier orders. What is the extent of this divergence? Where is your company located in the supply chain—is it toward the front of the chain close to the end customer or is it further toward the back of the chain? Remember, the distortion caused by divergence of incoming orders with outgoing orders increases as it moves back through the supply chain.

Many companies are not aware of the cost of the bullwhip effect on their supply chains. Traditionally, demand variability caused by the bullwhip effect was taken as a given and companies worked on their own to develop better capabilities to respond to fluctuations in demand. It may instead be far more efficient for companies to work together to actually reduce the fluctuations in demand. A company can either try to optimize its individual response to fluctuating demand or it can collaborate with other companies to reduce the fluctuations themselves.

Once you have established the magnitude of the bullwhip effect in your company, then get some estimates of the cost consequences in different areas of the company. What is the effect of this demand variability on production costs and scheduling? What is the effect on transportation costs and shipping and receiving costs? What inventory levels are needed to maintain service levels in such a volatile situation and what is the associated carrying cost? What is the effect on product availability and order lead times—are sales lost because of lack of inventory?

These estimates show the cost to the company of dealing with demand fluctuations. This is the basis upon which to discuss what it might be worth to fix the bullwhip effect.

EXECUTIVE INSIGHT

Why do we need universal product code (UPC) numbers? Because when each company uses only its own part number for the same product as it moves through the supply chain, what results is confusion and inefficiency.

Historically, companies have assigned their own part numbers to the items that they buy and sell. This worked well enough in a slower time when supply chains were less complex and when products themselves were less complex. Those were times we now refer to as the "good old days." Increasing competition and demands from customers to deliver products faster and cheaper shapes the world we live in today. At the same time, the array and complexity of products in our economy has increased dramatically and that trend will clearly continue and even accelerate.

In order to be competitive and also profitable, companies need to find ways to reduce or eliminate costs associated with routine and repetitive business transactions. Those transactions often fall in the areas of purchasing, billing, accounts receivable, and accounts payable. It is in these areas that the confusion caused by translating part numbers is most noticeable. Time spent translating one part number to another part number for the same item adds very little, if any, value to the transaction. The errors that result from errors in translation are the cause of many problems in invoicing and making payments. These problems consume people's time and slow down cash flow. All these expenses simply eat away at profit margins that are already thin enough.

In addition to the operating problems caused by using different part numbers for the same item, another consequence is a lack of accuracy and clarity in sales history data. Part number translation errors result in sales of some items being undercounted and sales of other items being overcounted. And sales of many items are simply not counted at all or they are lumped under a miscellaneous part number such as the famous "9999" part number. Sales history data is usually the basis for forecasting future demand and this fuzziness in the data hampers efforts to improve demand forecasts, production scheduling, and inventory management.

In order for companies to coordinate effectively, they need to have a single part number that stays with a part as it makes its way through the supply chain. That number is the Universal Product Code (UPC) number. Standards for the use of UPC numbers are set by the Uniform Code Council (www.uc-council.org). Companies that do business together need to be able to tag every item that they buy and sell with a UPC number. They can still use their internal part numbers for internal operations if they wish. But when they communicate with each other they need to use UPC numbers so as to eliminate the need to do part number translations. There are many more valuable and profitable things that can be done with the time and money that now goes into translating part numbers and dealing with translation-related problems.

The Integrated Business Communications Alliance or IBCA (www .ibcaweb.org) presents a short and useful white paper on this subject. The paper is titled "A Starting Place for eCommerce" and it presents a pragmatic and simple way for companies to get started. The white paper can be found on the IBCA web site and downloaded.

Information Systems that Support the Supply Chain

Information technology can support internal operations and also collaboration between companies in a supply chain. Using high speed data networks and databases, companies can share data to better manage the supply chain as a whole and their own individual positions within the supply chain. The effective use of this technology is a key aspect of a company's success.

All information systems are composed of technology that performs three main functions: data capture and communication; data storage and retrieval; and data manipulation and reporting. Different information systems have different combinations of capabilities in these functional areas. The specific combination of capabilities is dependent on the demands of the job that a system is designed to perform. Information systems that are employed to support various aspects of supply chain management are created from technologies that perform some combination of these functions.

Data Capture and Data Communications

The first functional area is composed of systems and technology that create high speed data capture and communications networks. It is this technology that can overcome the lag times and lack of big picture information that gives rise to the bullwhip effect. We will look at:

- The Internet
- Broadband
- EDI
- XML

The Internet

The Internet is the global data communications network that uses what is known as Internet Protocol (IP) standards to move data from one point to another. The Internet is the universal communications network that can connect with all computers and communication devices. Once a device is hooked into the Internet it can communicate with any other device that is also connected to the Internet regardless of the different internal data formats that they may use.

Before the Internet, companies had to put in expensive dedicated networks to connect themselves to other companies and move data between their different computer systems. Now, with the Internet already in place, different companies have a way to quickly and inexpensively connect their computer systems. If needed, extra data protection and privacy can be provided by using technology to create virtual private networks (VPNs) that utilize the Internet to create very secure communication networks.

Broadband

Basically, this means any communications technology that offers high speed (faster than a 56Kb dial-up modem) access to the Internet with a connection that is always on. This includes technologies such as coaxial cable, digital subscriber line (DSL), metro Ethernet, fixed wireless, and satellite. Broadband technology is spreading and as it does, it becomes possible for companies in a supply chain to easily and inexpensively hook up with each other and exchange large volumes of data in real-time.

Most companies have connected themselves internally using local area network (LAN) technology such as Ethernet that gives them plenty of internal communications capability. Many companies have connected some or all of their different geographical locations using wide area network (WAN) technology such as T1, T3, or frame relay. What now needs to happen is high speed, relatively low cost connections between separate companies and that is the role that broadband will play.

EDI

Electronic Data Interchange (EDI) is a technology that was developed to transmit common types of data between companies that do business with each other. It was first deployed in the 1980s by large companies in the manufacturing, automobile, and transportation industries. It was built to automate back office transactions such as the sending and receiving of purchase orders (known as an "850" transaction), invoices (an "810"), advance shipment notices (an "856"), and backorder status (an "855") to name just a few. It originally was built to run on big, mainframe computers using value added networks (VANs) to connect with other trading partners. That technology was expensive.

Many companies have large existing investments in EDI systems and find that it is very cost effective to continue to use these systems to communicate with other businesses. Standard EDI data sets have been defined for a large number of business transactions. Companies can decide which data sets they will use and which parts of each data set they will use. EDI systems can now run on any type of computer from mainframe to PC and it can use the Internet for data communications as well as VANs. Costs for EDI technology have come down considerably.

XML

XML (eXtensible Markup Language) is a technology that is being developed to transmit data in flexible formats between computers and between computers and humans. Where EDI uses rigid, pre-defined data sets to send data back and forth, XML is extensible and once certain standards have been agreed upon, XML can also be used to communicate a wide range of different kinds of data and related processing instructions between different computer systems. XML can also be used to communicate between computers and humans because it can drive user interfaces such as web browsers and respond to human input. Unlike EDI, the exact data transactions and processing sequences do not have to be previously defined when using XML.

There are many evolving XML standards in different industries but as yet none of these standards has been widely adopted. The industry that has made the most progress in adopting XML standards is the electronics industry. They are beginning to implement the RosettaNet XML standards (www.rosettanet.org).

In the near term, XML and EDI are merging into hybrid systems that are evolving to meet the needs of companies in different supply chains. It is not cost effective for companies with existing EDI systems that are working well enough to replace them with newer XML systems all at once. So XML extensions are being grafted onto EDI systems. Software is available to quickly translate EDI data to XML and then back to EDI. Service providers are now offering Internet-based EDI to smaller suppliers who do business with large EDI-using customers.

In the longer term, EDI will be wholly consumed by XML as XML standards are agreed upon and start to spread. As these standards spread they will enable very flexible communications between companies in a supply chain. XML will allow communications that are more spontaneous and free form, like any human language. This kind of communication will drive a network of computers and people interacting with other computers and other people. The purpose of this network will be to coordinate supply operations on a daily basis.

Data Storage and Retrieval

The second functional area of an information system is composed of technology that stores and retrieves data. This activity is performed by database technology. A database is an organized grouping of data that is stored in an electronic format. The most common type of database uses what is called "relational database" technology. Relational databases store related groups of data in individual tables and provide for retrieval of data with the use of a standard language called structured query language (SQL).

A database is a model of the business processes for which it collects and stores data. The model is defined by the level of detail in the data it collects. The design of every database has to strike a balance between highly aggregate data at one extreme and highly detailed data at the other extreme. This balance is arrived at by weighing the needs and budget of a business against the increasing cost associated with more and more detailed data. The balance is reflected in what is called the data model of the database.

As events occur in a business process, there are database transactions. The data model of the database determines which transactions can be recorded since the database cannot record transactions that are either more detailed or more aggregated than provided for in the data model. These transactions can be recorded as soon as they happen and that is called "real-time" updating or they may be captured and recorded in batches that happen on a periodic basis and that is called "batch" updating.

A database also provides for the different data retrieval needs of the people who use it. People doing different jobs will want different combinations of data from the same database. These different combinations are called "views." Views can be created and made available to people who need them to do their jobs. For instance, consider a database that contains sales history for a range of different products to a range of different customers. A customer view of this data might show a customer the different products and quantities they purchased over a period of time and show detail of the purchases at each customer location. A manufacturer view might show all the customers who bought their group of products over a period of time and show detail for the products that each customer bought.

Data Manipulation and Reporting

Different supply chain systems are created by combining processing logic to manipulate and display data with the technology required to capture, communicate, store, and retrieve data. The way that a system manipulates and displays the data that flows through it is determined by the specific business operations that the system is designed to support. Information systems contain the processing logic needed by the business operations they support. Chopra and Meindl define several kinds of systems that support supply chain operations:

- Enterprise Resource Planning (ERP)
- Procurement Systems
- Advanced Planning and Scheduling
- Transportation Planning Systems
- Demand Planning
- Customer Relation Management (CRM) and Sales Force Automation (SFA)
- Supply Chain Management (SCM)
- Inventory Management Systems
- Manufacturing Execution Systems (MES)
- Transportation Scheduling Systems
- Warehouse Management Systems (WMS)

Enterprise Resource Planning

Enterprise Resource Planning (ERP) systems gather data from across multiple functions in a company. ERP systems monitor orders, production schedules, raw material purchases, and finished goods inventory.

They support a process-oriented view of business that cuts across different functional departments. For instance, an ERP system can view the entire order fulfillment process and track an order from the procurement of material to fill the order to delivery of the finished product to the customer.

ERP systems come in modules that can be installed on their own or in combination with other modules. There are usually modules for finance, procurement, manufacturing, order fulfillment, human resources, and logistics. The focus of these modules is primarily on carrying out and monitoring daily transactions. ERP systems often lack the analytical capabilities needed to optimize the efficiency of these transactions.

Procurement Systems

Procurement systems focus on the procurement activities that take place between a company and its suppliers. The purpose of these systems is to streamline the procurement process and make it more efficient. Such systems typically replace supplier catalogs with a product database that contains all the needed information about products the company buys. They also keep track of part numbers, prices, purchasing histories, and supplier performance.

Procurement systems allow people to compare the price and performance capabilities of different suppliers. This way the best suppliers are identified so that relationships can be established with these suppliers and prices negotiated. The routine transactions that occur in the purchasing process can then be largely automated.

Advanced Planning and Scheduling

Advanced Planning and Scheduling, also known as APS systems, are highly analytical applications whose purpose is to assess plant capacity, material availability, and customer demand. These systems then produce schedules for what to make in which plant and at what time. APS systems base their calculations on the input of transaction level data that is extracted from ERP or legacy transaction processing systems. They then use linear programming techniques and other sophisticated algorithms to create their recommended schedules.

Transportation Planning Systems

Transportation Planning Systems are systems that calculate what quantity of materials should be brought to what locations at what times. The systems enable people to compare different modes of transportation, different routes, and different carriers. Transportation plans are then created using these systems. The software for these systems is sold by system vendors. Other providers known as content vendors provide the data that is needed by these systems, such as mileage, fuel costs, and shipping tariffs.

Demand Planning

These systems use special techniques and algorithms to help a company forecast their demand. These systems take historical sales data and information about planned promotions and other events that can affect customer demand, such as seasonality and market trends. They use this data to create models that help predict future sales.

Another feature that is often associated with demand planning systems is revenue management. This feature lets a company experiment with different price mixes for its different products in light of the predicted demand. The idea is to find a mix of products and prices that maximizes total revenue to the company. Companies in the travel industry such as airlines, rental car agencies, and hotels are already using revenue management techniques. These techniques will spread to other industries.

Customer Relation Management and Sales Force Automation

Systems of this type automate many of the tasks related to servicing existing customers and finding new customers. Customer Relation Management (CRM) systems track buying patterns and histories of customers. They consolidate a company's customer-related data in a place where it is quickly accessible to customer service and sales people who use the data to better respond to customer requests.

Sales Force Automation (SFA) systems allow a company to better coordinate and monitor the activities of its sales force. These systems automate many of the tasks related to scheduling sales calls and follow-up visits and preparing quotes and proposals for customers and prospects.

Supply Chain Management

Supply Chain Management (SCM) systems are suites of different supply chain applications, such as those described here that are tightly integrated with each other. An SCM system could be an integrated suite that contains advanced planning and scheduling, transportation planning, demand planning, and inventory planning applications. SCM systems rely on ERP or relevant legacy systems to provide them with the data to support the analysis and planning that they do. These systems have the analytical capabilities to support strategic level decision making.

Inventory Management Systems

These systems support the activities described in Chapter 2 that are part of inventory management such as tracking historical demand patterns for products, monitoring inventory levels for different products, and calculating economic order quantities and the levels of safety inventory that should be held for each product. These systems are used to find the right balance for a company between the cost of carrying inventory and the cost of running out of inventory and losing sales revenue because of that.

Manufacturing Execution Systems

The focus is on carrying out the production activities in a factory. This kind of system is less analytical than an APS. It produces short-term production schedules and allocates raw materials and production resources within a single manufacturing plant. A Manufacturing Execution System (MES) is similar in its operational focus to an ERP system and frequently MES software is produced by ERP software vendors.

Transportation Scheduling Systems

Systems in this category are similar to ERP and MES applications in that they are less analytical and more focused on daily operational issues. A transportation scheduling system produces short-term transportation and delivery schedules that are used by a company.

Warehouse Management Systems

These systems support daily warehouse operations. They provide capabilities to efficiently run the ongoing operations of a warehouse. These systems keep track of inventory levels and stocking locations within a warehouse and they support the actions needed to pick, pack, and ship product to fill customer orders.

Assessing Technology and System Needs

When evaluating different systems that can be used to support your supply chain it is important to keep in mind your goal—the reason for using any of these systems. Customers desire good service and good prices. That is what guides them when they select companies to do business with. Technology is a means for a company to be of service to its customers. Companies that keep this in mind do well.

In business, technology is only important insofar as it enables a company or an entire supply chain to deliver valuable products and services to its customers profitably. Do not let the complexity or the details of any technology or system be a distraction from this basic truth. Technology can be impressive but it is not an end in itself.

Success in supply chain management comes from delivering the highest levels of service at the lowest cost. Technology is expensive and can quickly add a lot of cost to a business. It is a far better thing to use simple technology well than to use sophisticated technology in a clumsy manner.

EXECUTIVE INSIGHT

Starting in the late 1990s supply chain service providers have sprung up to handle the needs of many specific markets. There has been a high turnover in these companies as the markets have evolved. Those companies that have survived are now focused on providing specific services to well-defined groups of customers.

Tibersoft (www.Tibersoft.com) provides order management services and supply chain monitoring and analysis systems to companies in the food and the maintenance supplies industries. Christopher Martin is the Vice Chairman and founder of Tibersoft. "Order management is simple, but difficult to execute well. The supply chains we serve are very high velocity and mistakes are costly. Order management systems are the pinion gears used to keep everything moving smoothly."

With the Internet, order management systems now span multiple companies in a supply chain. Their primary function is to present customers with the information they need to place orders and then communicate the orders to the companies that will fulfil them. This extended supply chain requires tight integration between the order management system and various internal systems in companies that are part of the supply chain. Chris explained, "You are always updating data about product, price, and promotion. Strong integration with back office systems is crucial. Our systems are extensions of the buyers' and the sellers' back office systems linked together over the Internet.

"Once you've taken the order there is a lot of tracking of that order to let people know about things like order status, backorders and substitutions, advance ship notices. The velocity in supply chains is definitely increasing and people want increasing control over their supply chains because of this."

The last few years have provided more understanding about the kind of control that people want. Chris continued, "There was a movement a couple of years ago where companies tried to create automated responses to supply chain events. That stopped because people didn't want technology to run the supply chain, they want technology to spot exceptions and bring them to their attention. This requires the order management system to get a continuous data feed from other systems. The data needed cannot be provided by manual input.

"People who are successful with Internet technology have learned that improving business is a series of incremental steps. They are totally focused on solving a specific problem. Supply chain service providers that focus on specific processes within well-defined vertical markets are the ones who will succeed. You have to go deep into the business processes of your customers to really advance the state of the art. Companies that try to do many functions across a range of markets just skim the surface and cannot provide enough value to deliver a compelling ROI."

When discussing the growth strategy of the company, Chris referred to a lesson he learned from a mentor, Max Hopper, "Scope drives scale and scale drives scope." He continued, "What he means is that we need to start with the scope of our existing products and go for as much scale as possible. Get as much business as we can. Customers will then tell you what they want in the next version—and we go again to build up the scale. We have come to believe that if a customer feels strongly enough that they will pay for a new feature, only then is it worth building that feature. Purely speculative development is a pernicious habit. Frankly, we don't waste a lot of time trying to revolutionize an industry. We work with individual customers to give them what they need to achieve their individual ROIs. The art is combining these solutions into the same code base."

Chris summed up what the last several years have taught them, "We don't want to rebuild systems that are already out there. We are here to connect these different systems and provide the data across the extended supply chain. Tibersoft does this by building private, point-to-point connections between companies using common data protocols. And those connections need to remain just that—private. Many dot com companies got themselves in trouble taking the data generated between their customers and using it to their economic benefit. "Enable, don't participate: that rule we don't break."

E-Business and Supply Chain Integration

The widespread availability and use of the Internet offers companies opportunities that did not exist before. These opportunities are made possible because it is now so easy and relatively inexpensive for companies to connect to the Internet. Once connected, companies can send data to and receive data from other companies that they do business with regardless of the particular computers or software that individual companies may be using to run their internal operations. Based on this data sharing, opportunities exist to achieve tremendous supply chain efficiencies and significant increases in customer service and responsiveness. These are the results of better supply chain integration.

E-business encompasses the evolving set of principles and practices that companies are employing to gain the benefits inherent in better supply chain integration. In the words of Professors Hau Lee and Seungjin Whang of Stanford University, e-business specifically refers to, "the planning and execution of the front-end and back-end operations in a supply chain using the Internet."

In a white paper titled "E-Business and Supply Chain Integration" published by the Stanford Global Supply Chain Management Forum (www.stanford.edu/group/scforum/) professors Lee and Whang lay out four key dimensions of the impact of e-business on supply chain integration. These four dimensions create a sequence of greater and greater integration and coordination among supply chain participants. This sequence culminates in the creation of whole new ways to conduct business. The four dimensions are:

1. *Information integration*—Is the ability to share relevant information among companies in a supply chain. This includes data such as: sales history and demand forecasts; inventory status; production schedules; production capacities; sales promotions; and transportation schedules. This data should be available to the people who need it in a real-time, on-line format via the Internet or private network.

2. *Planning synchronization*—Refers to the joint participation of companies in a supply chain in the demand forecasting and inventory replenishment scheduling. It also includes the collaborative design, development, and bringing to market of new products.

3. *Workflow coordination*—Is the next step after planning synchronization. It is the streamlining and automation of ongoing business activities across companies in a given supply chain. This includes activities such as purchasing and product design.

4. *New business models*—Can emerge as a result of supply chain integration made possible by the Internet. Roles and responsibilities

of companies in a supply chain can be redesigned so that each company can truly concentrate on the activities that are its core competencies. Non-core activities can be outsourced to other companies. New capabilities and efficiencies will become possible.

Experience of the Last Several Years

Several waves of e-business development have occurred since the late 1990s. The first wave of developments by entrepreneurial start-up companies typically focused on using Internet-based exchanges to improve purchasing efficiencies and drive down the cost of products through the use of online bid/auction techniques. Then industry news, statistics, and reference material were added to many of these exchanges and they were referred to as industry portals. Most of these developments have not lived up to expectations.

The next wave of developments continued to focus on purchasing efficiencies but this time the systems were developed by the purchasing companies themselves instead of by third party entrepreneurs. Often these developments have taken the form of a consortium of big companies in an industry banding together to finance the start up of an Internet-based purchasing platform that will support the whole range of their purchasing functions. Examples of this are Covisint in the automobile industry, ForestExpress in the forest products industry, and Aero Exchange International in the airline industry. These developments are yielding efficiencies in procurement operations.

The most recent wave of developments are now looking at how to achieve efficiencies in a broad range of supply chain operations such as product design, demand forecasting, inventory management, and customer service. The key to realizing these efficiencies is information sharing between companies in a supply chain. Many current e-business developments are working on methods and standards to share information across multiple companies. Information sharing is the foundation and then cross-company coordination is what will deliver the desired efficiencies. Once information integration is in place, the next three dimensions: planning synchronization; workflow coordination; and new business models can evolve much more rapidly. E-business development has only just begun.

Chapter Summary

One of the most common dynamics in supply chains is a phenomena that has been dubbed "the bullwhip effect." What happens is that small changes in product demand by the consumer at the front of the supply chain translate into wider and wider swings in demand as experienced by companies further back in the supply chain. Companies at different stages in the supply chain come to have very different pictures of market demand and the result is a breakdown in supply chain coordination. Companies behave in ways that at first create product shortages and then lead to an excess supply of product.

Many companies are not aware of the cost of the bullwhip effect on their supply chains. Traditionally, demand variability caused by the bullwhip effect was taken as a given and companies worked on their own to develop better capabilities to respond to fluctuations in demand. It may instead be far more efficient for companies to work together to actually reduce the fluctuations in demand. A company can either try to optimize its individual response to fluctuating demand or it can collaborate with other companies to reduce the fluctuations themselves.

The use of supporting technology is necessary for effective supply chain operations. All information systems are composed of technology that performs three main functions: data capture and communication; data storage and retrieval; and data manipulation and reporting. Different supply chain information systems have different combinations of capabilities in these functional areas.

CHAPTER 5

Measuring Performance: Supply Chain Metrics

After reading this chapter you will be able to

- Employ a useful model for assessing markets and the supply chains that support them

- Define a concise set of metrics for measuring the performance of a company's supply chain operations

- Discuss ways to collect and display supply chain performance data

- Use performance data to spotlight problems and opportunities

Supply chains are fluid and are continuously adjusting to changes in supply and demand for the products they handle. To get the performance desired from supply chains requires a company to monitor and control its operations on a daily basis. This chapter introduces four performance categories that each supply chain participant should measure. It then discusses the performance metrics that can be used in each of these performance categories. The chapter also explores some of the technology that can be used to collect, store, and present performance data.

A Useful Model of Markets and Their Supply Chains

A supply chain exists to support the market that it serves. To identify the performance that a supply chain should deliver, we need to evaluate the market being served. In support of this analysis we will employ a simple model. The model allows us to categorize a market and identify the requirements and opportunities that each kind of market presents to its supply chains. Reality is, of course, more subtle and more complex than any model can represent but this model can point you in the right direction and guide you through an investigation of the markets your company serves.

Let us start by defining a market using its two most basic components— supply and demand. A market is characterized by its combination of supply and demand. This model defines four basic kinds of markets, or market quadrants. In the first quadrant is a market where both supply and demand for its products are low and unpredictable. Let's call this a *developing* market. In the second quadrant is a market where supply is low and demand is high. This is a *growth* market. The third quadrant contains a market where both supply and demand are high. There is a lot of predictability in this market so call this a *steady* market. In the fourth quadrant, this kind of market supply is higher than demand. This is a *mature* market.

In a developing market, both supply and demand are low and also uncertain. These are usually new markets that are just emerging. These markets are created by new technology becoming available or by social and economic trends that cause a group of customers to perceive some new set of needs. Opportunities in a developing market are in the areas of partnering with other players in the supply chain to gather intelligence about what the market wants. Cost of sales is high in this market and inventories are low.

Growth markets are markets where demand is higher than supply and so supply is often uncertain. If a developing market solidifies and builds up momentum, it can suddenly take off and for a time there is a surge in demand that suppliers cannot keep up with. Opportunities in a growth market are in providing a high level of customer service as measured by order fill rates and on-time deliveries. Customers in a market like this value a reliable source of supply and will pay premium prices for reliability. Cost of sales should be low since customers are easy to find and inventories can be higher because they are increasing in value.

In a steady market both supply and demand are high and thus relatively predictable. This is an established market where market forces have been at work for a while and have pretty well balanced supply and demand. Opportunities here lie in fine tuning and optimizing internal company operations. Companies should focus on minimizing inventory and cost of sales while maintaining high levels of customer service.

In a mature market, supply has overtaken demand and excess supply capacity exists. Demand is reasonably stable or slowly falling but because of the fierce competition due to oversupply, demand seems uncertain from the point of view of any one supplier in this market. Opportunities in this market are in the area of flexibility as measured by an ability to respond quickly to changes in product demand while maintaining high levels of customer service. Customers in a market like this value the convenience of "one stop shopping" where they can purchase a wide variety of related products at low prices. Inventories should be minimized and the cost of sales are somewhat higher due to the expense of attracting customers in a crowded market.

Market Performance Categories

Markets in each quadrant have their own mix of opportunities for the supply chains that support them. A different mix of performance characteristics is required of companies in the supply chains of each kind of market. In order to thrive, the companies in a supply chain must be able to work together to exploit the opportunities available in their markets. The highest profits go to the companies that can successfully respond to

Each Market Quadrant Presents Different Opportunities

MATURE	**STEADY**
Supply exceeds demand	Established market, supply and demand are balanced
Opportunities lie in coordinating with supply chain partners to provide a wide range of products to the market and accommodate wide fluctuations in product demand while maintaining high levels of customer service.	Opportunities lie in each company fine tuning and optimizing their internal operations to get maximum efficiency and best overall supply chain profitability.
DEVELOPING	**GROWTH**
New market and new products, supply and demand are low	Demand exceeds supply
Opportunities lie in partnering with other companies in the supply chain to gather intelligence about what the market wants and build and deliver products that will be attractive to the market.	Opportunities lie in building market share and recognition through working with supply chain partners to provide high levels of customer service as measured by order fill rate and on-time delivery.

SUPPLY

DEMAND ⟶

What are the markets your company serves? What quadrants are they in? How can your company respond to the opportunities in these markets?

the opportunities their markets offer. Companies that are unable to respond to opportunities as effectively will fall behind.

In Chapter 1 we introduced two characteristics that describe supply chain performance—responsiveness and efficiency. We all intuitively know what these two characteristics imply, but now we need to define them in more precise terms so that they can be measured objectively. We will use four measurement categories:

1. Customer Service

2. Internal Efficiency

3. Demand Flexibility

4. Product Development

Customer Service

Customer service measures the ability of the supply chain to meet the expectations of its customers. Depending on the type of market being served, the customers in that market will have different expectations for customer service. Customers in some markets both expect and will pay for high levels of product availability and quick delivery of small purchase quantities. Customers in other markets will accept longer waits for products and will purchase in large quantities. Whatever the market being served, the supply chain must meet the customer service expectations of the people in that market.

Internal Efficiency

Internal efficiency refers to the ability of a company or a supply chain to operate in such a way as to generate an appropriate level of profitability. As with customer service, market conditions vary and what is an appropriate level of profit varies from one market to another. In a risky developing market the profit margins need to be higher in order to justify the investment of time and money. In a mature market where there is little uncertainty or risk, profit margins can be somewhat lower. These markets offer the opportunity to do large volumes of business and to make up in gross profit what is given up in gross margin.

Demand Flexibility

This category measures the ability to respond to uncertainty in levels of product demand. It shows how much of an increase over current levels of demand can be handled by a company or a supply chain. It also includes the ability to respond to uncertainty in the range of products that may be demanded. This ability is often needed in mature markets.

Product Development

This encompasses a company and a supply chain's ability to continue to evolve along with the markets it serves. It measures the ability to develop and deliver new products in a timely manner. This ability is necessary when serving developing markets.

A Framework for Performance Measurement

There are other demands that real-world markets place on their supply chains, however, by using these four performance categories we can create a useful framework. This framework describes the mix of performance required from companies and supply chains that serve the four different market quadrants. When a company identifies the markets it serves it can then define the performance mix required by those markets in order to best respond to the opportunities they provide.

Markets in the first quadrant, developing markets, require their supply chains to excel in product development and customer service. Growth markets require very high levels of customer service particularly as measured by order fill rates and on-time delivery. Steady markets require internal efficiency as well as an even broader scope of customer service. Mature markets require all the internal efficiency and customer service called for by steady markets. They also require the highest levels of demand flexibility.

The most profitable companies and supply chains are those that deliver the performance called for by their markets. These organizations are the most profitable because they are the ones most able to respond effectively to the opportunities offered by their markets. Companies should collect and track a handful of performance measures that cover these four areas. This will give them valuable information about how well they are responding to their markets.

The metrics that measure performance in the four areas are applicable to individual companies and also to entire supply chains. It is harder to gather these metrics for entire supply chains because companies are reluctant to share data that may be used against them by their competitors or by their customers or suppliers. There are issues of trust and incentive

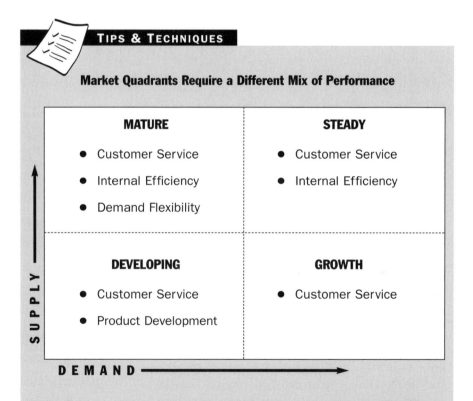

TIPS & TECHNIQUES

Market Quadrants Require a Different Mix of Performance

MATURE	**STEADY**
• Customer Service	• Customer Service
• Internal Efficiency	• Internal Efficiency
• Demand Flexibility	
DEVELOPING	**GROWTH**
• Customer Service	• Customer Service
• Product Development	

SUPPLY

DEMAND ⟶

Does your company excel in the performance categories that relate to the markets you serve? Profit opportunities lie in being a leader in the mix of performance categories that your markets call for.

to work out before these metrics can readily be collected for an entire supply chain. Nonetheless, when these issues are worked out, these metrics will help to guide the behavior of the entire supply chain and should benefit all the participants in that chain over the long term.

Customer Service Metrics

In the words of Warren Hausman, a professor at Stanford University, "service relates to the ability to anticipate, capture and fulfill customer demand with personalized products and on-time delivery" (Hausman, Warren H., 2000, "Supply Chain Performance Metrics," Management Science & Engineering Department, Stanford University). The reason that any company exists is to be of service to its customers. The reason that any supply chain exists is to serve the market it is attached to. These measures indicate how well a company serves its customers and how well a supply chain supports its market.

There are two sets of customer service metrics depending on whether the company or supply chain is in a build to stock (BTS) or build to order (BTO) situation. Popular metrics for a build to stock situation are:

- Complete Order Fill Rate and Order Line Item Fill Rate
- On-Time Delivery Rate
- Value of Total Backorders and Number of Backorders
- Frequency and Duration of Backorders
- Line Item Return Rate

Popular metrics for a build to order situation are:

- Quoted Customer Response Time and On-Time Completion Rate
- On-Time Delivery Rate
- Value of Late Orders and Number of Late Orders
- Frequency and Duration of Late Orders
- Number of Warranty Returns and Repairs

Build to Stock

A build to stock or BTS situation is one where common commodity products are supplied to a large market or customer base. These are products such as office supplies, cleaning supplies, building supplies, and so on. Customers expect to get these products right away any time they need them. Supply chains for these products must meet this demand by stocking them in inventory so they are always available.

In a BTS environment a customer wants their complete order to be filled immediately. This may be expensive to provide if customer orders contain a wide range and number of items. It is costly for companies to carry all those items in stock so they may have backup plans to provide expedited delivery of items not in stock or substitution of upgraded items for those not in stock. The order fill rate measures the percentage of total orders where all items on the order are filled immediately from stock. The line item fill rate is the percentage of total line items on all orders that are filled immediately from stock. Used together, these two measures track customer service from two important perspectives.

Build to Order

A build to order or BTO situation is one where a customized product is ordered by a customer. This is any situation where a product is built based on a specific customer order and is configured to meet a unique set of requirements defined by the customer. An example of this is the way Boeing builds airplanes for specific customers and their requirements or the way Dell Computer assembles PCs to fit individual customer orders and specifications.

In a BTO environment it is important to track both the quoted customer response time and the on-time completion rate. It is easier for a company to achieve a high on-time completion rate if it quotes longer customer response times. The question is whether the customer really wants a short response time or will accept a longer response time. The quoted response time needs to be aligned with the company's value proposition and competitive strategy.

Internal Efficiency Metrics

Internal efficiency refers to the ability of a company or a supply chain to use their assets as profitably as possible. Assets include anything of tangible value such as plant, equipment, inventory, and cash. Some popular measures of internal efficiency are:

- Inventory value
- Inventory turns
- Return on sales
- Cash-to-cash cycle time

Inventory Value

This should be measured both at a point in time and also as an average over time. The major asset involved in a supply chain is the inventory contained throughout the length of the chain. Supply chains and the companies that make them up are always looking for ways to reduce inventory while still delivering high levels of customer service. This means trying to match inventory availability (supply) with sales (demand) and not have excess inventory left over. The only time a company would want to let inventory exceed sales is in a growth market where the value of the inventory will increase. However, markets change and as a rule it is best to avoid excess inventory.

Inventory Turns

This is a way to measure the profitability of inventory by tracking the speed with which it is sold or turned over during the course of a year. This measure is often referred to as T & E or "turn and earn." It is calculated by the equation:

Turns = Annual Cost of Sales / Annual Average Inventory Value

Generally, the higher the turn rate the better, although some lower turning inventory needs to be available in order to meet customer service and demand flexibility.

Return on Sales

Return on sales is a broad measure of how well an operation is being run. It measures how well fixed and variables costs are managed and also the gross profit generated on sales:

Return on Sales = Earnings before Interest & Tax / Sales

Again, as a rule, the higher the return on sales the better. There are times though when a company may deliberately reduce this number in order to gain or defend market share or to incur expenses that are necessary to achieve some other business objective.

Cash-to-Cash Cycle Time

This is the time it takes from when a company pays its suppliers for materials to when it gets paid by its customers. This time can be estimated with the following formula:

Cash-to-Cash Cycle Time = Inventory Days of Supply +
Days Sales Outstanding – Average Payment Period on Purchases

The shorter this cycle time the better. A company can often make more improvements in their accounts payable and receivable areas than they can in their inventory levels. Accounts receivable may be large due to late payments caused by billing errors or selling to customers who are bad credit risks. These are things a company can manage as well as inventory.

Demand Flexibility Metrics

Demand flexibility describes a company's ability to be responsive to new demands in the quantity and range of products and to act quickly. A company or supply chain needs capabilities in this area in order to cope with uncertainty in the markets they serve. Some measures of flexibility are:

- Activity Cycle Time
- Upside Flexibility
- Outside Flexibility

Activity Cycle Time

The cycle time measures the amount of time it takes to perform a supply chain activity such as order fulfillment, product design, product assembly, or any other activity that supports the supply chain. This cycle time can be measured within an individual company or across an entire supply chain. Order fulfillment within a single company may be fast but that company may only be filling an order from another company in the supply chain. What is important is the cycle time for order fulfillment to the ultimate end use customer that the entire supply chain is there to serve.

Upside Flexibility

It is the ability of a company or supply chain to respond quickly to additional order volume for the products they carry. Normal order volume may be 100 units per week for a product. Can an order be accommodated that is 25 percent greater one week or will the extra product demand wind up as a backorder? Upside flexibility can be measured as the percentage increase over the expected demand for a product that can be accommodated.

Performance Measures in the Four Categories

CUSTOMER SERVICE

Build to Stock (BTS)

- Complete order fill rate & order line item fill rate

- On-time delivery rate

- Value of total backorders & number of backorders

- Frequency and duration of backorders

- Line item return rate

Build to Order (BTO)

- Quoted customer response time & on-time completion rate

- On-time delivery rate

- Value of late orders & number of late orders

- Frequency and duration of late orders

- Number of warranty returns and repairs

INTERNAL EFFICIENCY

- Inventory value

- Inventory turns

- Return on sales

- Cash-to-cash cycle time

DEMAND FLEXIBILITY

- Activity cycle times

- Upside flexibility

- Outside flexibility

PRODUCT DEVELOPMENT

- Percent of total sales from products introduced in last 12 months

- Percent of total SKUs that were introduced in last 12 months

- Cycle time for new product development and delivery

Companies need to track some or all of these metrics to get an accurate picture of their capabilities in the four performance categories.

Outside Flexibility

This is the ability to quickly provide the customer with additional products outside the bundle of products normally provided. As markets mature and technologies blend, products that were once considered outside of the range of a company's offerings can become a logical extension of its offerings. There is danger in trying to provide customers with a new and unrelated set of products that has little in common with the existing product bundle. However, there is opportunity to acquire new customers and sell more to existing customers when outside flexibility is managed skillfully.

Product Development Metrics

Product development measures a company or a supply chain's ability to design, build, and deliver new products to serve their markets as those markets evolve over time. Technical innovations, social change, and economic developments cause a market to change over time. Measurements in this performance category are often overlooked, but companies do so at their own peril. A supply chain must keep pace with the market it serves or it will be replaced. The ability to keep pace with an evolving market can be measured by metrics such as:

- Percentage of total products sold that were introduced in the last year

- Percentage of total sales from products introduced in the last year

- Cycle time to develop and deliver a new product

Operations that Enable Supply Chain Performance

In order for an organization to meet the performance requirements of the markets it serves it must look to measure and improve its capabilities in the four categories of supply chain operations:

1. Plan

2. Source

3. Make

4. Deliver

The efficiency with which these activities are carried out will ultimately determine how well a company performs as measured by things such as order and line item fill rate, on-time delivery, inventory turns,

EXECUTIVE INSIGHT

Measuring performance is a process of selecting a handful of meaningful indicators and using them to track company performance. Often the indicators are financial performance measurements.

Bob Mitchum is the CFO of a cooperative of distribution companies that serves customers across North America. This organization is called Network Services (www.nsconline.com). Bob is the one who keeps tabs on the performance of the organization as a whole and also of the member companies individually. All member companies need to meet several performance targets in order to remain members in good standing. This ensures that they are able to deliver the products and services demanded by Network Services' national account customers.

Bob watches four financial indicators of each member company's internal efficiency. Two of them measure the company's operating efficiency and two of them measure its resiliency—its ability to withstand tough times and respond to opportunities. "Over a 2-to-3 year period these ratios give a pretty clear picture of what's going on with a company. Network requires its members to meet or exceed the benchmark measures in these two areas as set by our industry trade association [National Paper Trade Association]." These financial indicators are:

Operating Efficiency

- *Return on Sales*—Pretax earnings (EBIT) as a percentage of sales

- *Return on Shareholder Equity*—EBIT as a percentage of shareholder equity

Resiliency

- *Debt to Net Worth*—Total debt divided by net worth

- *Interest Coverage*—EBIT divided by interest expense

Return on sales is an indicator of how well a business is being run. "It tells you if a company is operating within its means. If this number is going up year to year that means the company is getting more efficient. If the number is going down or becomes negative, that tells you the company is spending more than it is bringing in."

Return on shareholder equity shows how efficiently the company's money is being spent, "the higher this number the better." If a company cannot produce a return on equity that is better than putting that same money into a CD then the investors in that company need to question how well their money is being spent.

Debt to net worth measures a company's ability to borrow money and also how well the owners are leveraging their equity. "If the debt to equity ratio is high, then the company cannot borrow more money to either get through hard times or take advantage of an opportunity. At the same time, many owners of private companies like to have as high a ratio as possible, especially during times of low interest rates, because this means the owner is leveraging his risk by using the bank's money and not his own."

Interest coverage indicates how much additional money a company can borrow. "This shows how much additional interest on debt can be covered by a company's cash flow."

and cash-to-cash cycle time. Certain activities are directly related to certain performance categories. For instance, inventory management will directly affect a company's order and line item fill rate and its inventory turns. Its procurement activity will directly affect its return on sales and its upside ability. A company needs to collect data about its activities in these four operational areas and monitor results.

The Supply-Chain Council's SCOR model suggests the kind of operational data that should be collected. This data is referred to as "Level 2 Performance Metrics." In the plan operation, useful measures are the cost of planning activities, inventory financing costs, inventory days of supply on hand, and forecast accuracy. In the sourcing operation, it is useful to have data on material acquisition costs, sourcing cycle times, and raw material days of supply. Useful measures in the make operation are the number of product defects/complaints, make cycle times, build order attainment rates, and product quality. Suggested delivery operation measures are fill rates, order management costs, order lead times, and item return rates.

This data should be collected regularly and trends should be watched. When performance targets start to be missed, the next step is to investigate the business operations that support that performance. Again the SCOR model suggests more detailed data that can be collected and analyzed in each of the four supply chain operating areas. This more detailed data is referred to as "Level 3 Diagnostic Metrics."

Diagnostic metrics can be used to analyze the complexity and configuration of the supply chain and also to study specific practices. In the plan operation, complexity measures are the number and percentage of order changes, number of stock keeping units (SKUs) carried, production volumes, and inventory carrying costs. Configuration measures track things such as product volume by channel, number of channels, and number of supply chain locations. Measures of management practices

TIPS & TECHNIQUES

Business Operations
Support Company Performance

PERFORMANCE CATEGORIES / BUSINESS OPERATIONS	CUSTOMER SERVICE As measured by: Fill Rate; On-Time Delivery; Product Returns	INTERNAL EFFICIENCY As measured by: Inventory Turns; Return on Sales; Cash-to-Cash	DEMAND FLEXIBILITY As measured by: Cycle Times; Upside Flex; Outside Flex	PRODUCT DEVELOPMENT As measured by: New Prod Sales; % Revenue; Cycle Time
PLAN — Demand Forecast	X	X	X	
PLAN — Product Pricing	X	X		
PLAN — Inventory Management	X	X	X	
SOURCE — Procurement		X	X	
SOURCE — Credit & Collections	X	X		
MAKE — Product Design	X			X
MAKE — Production Scheduling		X	X	
MAKE — Facility Management	X	X		
DELIVER — Order Management	X	X		X
DELIVER — Delivery Scheduling	X	X		

in the plan operation are such things as planning cycle time, forecast accuracy, and obsolete inventory on hand.

In the source operation, measures of complexity and configuration are number of suppliers, percentage of purchasing spending by distance, and purchased material by geography. Some practice measurements are supplier delivery performance, payment period, and percentage of items purchased by their associated lead time.

The make operation has measures of complexity and configuration such as number of SKUs, upside production flexibility, manufacturing process steps by geographical location, and capacity utilization. Management practice measurements are value added percentage, build to order percentage, build to stock percentage, percentage of manufacturing order changes due to internal issues, and work in process inventory.

In the fourth supply chain operation, deliver, there are complexity measures that include number of orders by channel, number of line items and shipments by channel, and percentage of line items returned. Configuration measures are delivery locations by geography and number of channels. Practice measures cover things like published delivery lead times, percentage of invoices that contain billing errors, and order entry methods.

Collecting and Displaying Performance Data

Historically, companies based their management decisions on periodic, standard reports that showed what happened during some period in the past. In stable and slow-moving business environments this worked well enough. However, there are not many companies that work in stable and slow-moving environments any more. Working from traditional, periodic, accounting-oriented reports in a fast-paced world is somewhat like trying to drive a car by looking into the rear-view mirror.

The business environments we live in are characterized by shorter product life cycles, mass markets dissolving into smaller niche markets, and new technology and distribution channels constantly opening up new opportunities. The pace of change is both exhilarating and relentless. A company must keep up. To do this, a company needs to build a reporting system that presents data at three levels of detail:

- *Strategic*—to help top management decide *what* to do
- *Tactical*—to help middle management decide *how* to do it
- *Operational*—to help people *actually* do it

TIPS & TECHNIQUES

Supply Chain Performance Metrics and Diagnostic Measures (Supply-Chain Council SCOR Model)

	LEVEL 2	LEVEL 3		
	Performance Metrics	Complexity Measures	Configuration Measures	Practice Measures
P L A N	• Planning costs • Financing costs • Inventory days of supply	• % of order changes • # of SKUs carried • Production volume • Inventory carrying costs	• Product volume by channel • # of channels • # of supply chain locations	• Planning cycle time • Forecast accuracy • Obsolete inventory on hand
S O U R C E	• Material acquisition costs • Source cycle time • Raw material days of supply	• # of suppliers • % of purchasing spending by distance	• Purchased material by geography • % of purchasing spending by distance	• Supplier delivery performance • Payment period • % of items purchased by their associated lead times
M A K E	• # of defects or complaints • Make cycle time • Build order attainment • Product quality	• # of SKUs • Upside production flexibility	• Manufacturing process steps by geography • Capacity utilization	• Value add % • Build to order % • Build to stock % • % mfg. order changes due to internal issues • WIP inventory
D E L I V E R	• Fill rates • Order management costs • Order fulfillment lead times • Line item return rates	• # of orders by channel • # of line items and shipments by channel • % of line items returned	• Delivery locations by geography • # of channels	• Published delivery lead times • % invoices containing billing errors • Order entry methods

Three Levels of Detail

In a supply chain management context, strategic data consists of current actual, as well as plan and historical numbers that show the company's standing in the four performance categories: customer service; internal efficiency; demand flexibility; and product development. In the Supply-Chain Council SCOR model, data of this type is referred to as "Level 1" data. This data is summarized by major business units and for the company as a whole. Strategic data also consists of data from outside the company such as market sizes and growth rates, demographics, and economic indicators such as GNP, inflation rates, and interest rates. There should also be benchmark data from industry trade associations and studies that show the operating standards and financial performance levels that are standard for companies in the markets being served.

Tactical data consists of actual, plan, and historical numbers in the four performance categories displayed at the branch office level of detail. This data also includes the performance metrics labeled "Level 2" in the SCOR model. These metrics monitor the plan, source, make, and deliver operations that every company in a supply chain must perform.

Operational data consists of the measures labeled "Level 3" in the SCOR model. These measurements help people who are charged with getting a job done to understand what is happening and to find ways to make improvements where needed to meet the performance targets that have been set. The SCOR model refers to these measurements as diagnostic measures.

We are awash in data. It is important to present it in such a way that it is useful. If people are overwhelmed with data they cannot use it. By organizing data into these three levels, people can quickly access what they need to do their jobs. Upper management uses strategic level data to assess market conditions and set business performance objectives. They can drill down to the tactical level or even the operational levels when necessary. Middle managers use tactical data to do planning and resource allocation to achieve the performance objectives set by upper management. Line managers and their staffs use operational data to solve problems and get things done.

The Data Warehouse

To collect this data requires the creation of a data warehouse. This data warehouse is a central repository of data that is drawn from a variety of operating systems and accounting systems in a company. It is important to collect the needed data at its source. Tap into relevant systems within a company and capture needed data automatically as a by-product of daily operations. Avoid having people do manual entry to get data into the data warehouse.

A data warehouse is composed of a database software package and the automated connections to other systems needed to collect the relevant data on a regular and timely schedule. Working in conjunction with the database software is software that allows for the creation of standard predefined reports and graphic displays which people can use to monitor operations. In addition to predefined reports and displays, the software must also allow people to do ad hoc queries of the data in the data warehouse to do detailed investigations when necessary.

When designing and building a data warehouse it is best to start quickly with something that is simple and on a smaller scale. This way people can get experience in using data more actively to do their jobs. As they gain experience and can clearly describe the additional features they would like, larger and more complex data warehouses can be built. Remember, the most important component in any data warehouse system is not the technology, or even the data, but the people who use the system and their ability to use the system effectively and learn from the data and become more efficient at their jobs. Chapter 6 goes into further detail about the design and building of these kinds of systems.

In addition to helping people inside of a company to become more efficient in performing their supply chain management jobs, a data warehouse can also be the foundation for collaboration with other companies in the supply chain. Whatever information is shared between companies in a supply chain should be made available to those other companies electronically. This often takes the form of reports that can be retrieved on demand by other companies who access a company's data warehouse over the Internet using features of the same data reporting software that people inside the company use. See Exhibit 5.1.

Spotlighting Problems and Finding Opportunities

Depending on the type of markets a company serves, senior management needs to define a handful of key performance targets in the areas of customer service, internal efficiency, demand flexibility, and product development. The task then becomes one of figuring out how to manage operations to achieve the target numbers. The point of collecting performance data is to help monitor and control daily, weekly, and monthly operations.

People in a company need access to a one page display of the key operating or financial measures that they are responsible for achieving. These one page displays are known as "dashboards" because they show a person at a glance the data that is most important to them. The data that is displayed on a senior management dashboard is different from that on an operating manager's dashboard and the data on the dashboard of a staff person in one department is different from a staff person's in another department.

Senior management sets company performance targets and they need access to a dashboard report that shows them the company's current

EXHIBIT 5.1

Display Different Views of Data to Different Audiences

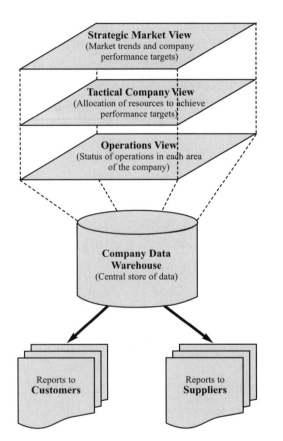

Strategic Market View
(Market trends and company performance targets)

Tactical Company View
(Allocation of resources to achieve performance targets)

Operations View
(Status of operations in each area of the company)

Company Data Warehouse
(Central store of data)

Reports to
Customers

Reports to
Suppliers

The data warehouse supports views of data at the strategic, tactical, and operational levels. This makes it easy for management and staff in a company to get quick access to the data they need to do their jobs. The data warehouse also supports the sharing of data with customers and suppliers needed to coordinate supply chain activities.

performance against these targets. If things are going well and performance is meeting expectations, then no further attention is called for, but if performance is falling short against one or more of the performance targets, then the senior manager knows right away where more attention is needed.

Middle managers are responsible for managing their operations to achieve one or more of the company's performance targets. Their dashboards need to show them the plan and actual data on company performance targets they are responsible for. They need to see quickly if operations are on target or not and direct their attention accordingly. Once alerted by their dashboard that there is a problem in a particular area, the manager can then drill down into further detail in that area.

Staff people in various departments need dashboards that track and illuminate the specific business operations that they are responsible for such as purchasing, credit, inventory management, and so on. These displays should highlight issues needing their attention.

For the most part, people run their business or do their job by keeping track of a handful of key indicators. These indicators tell them where to direct their attention and help them steer through a complex and changing world. When a data warehouse and software reporting tools are in place in a company, people need to experiment with the design of their dashboard displays or reports. As they get better at using their dashboards to guide their actions, the overall effect will be for the company as a whole to become more efficient and more responsive to its markets.

Since very few companies work in stable and slow-moving markets anymore, there is a great need to learn to use data effectively to make decisions and act. Speed is a major competitive advantage. The faster a company can spot problems and fix them or see opportunities and respond to them, the more profitable the company will be. It will also have a much better chance of survival over the long term. Companies

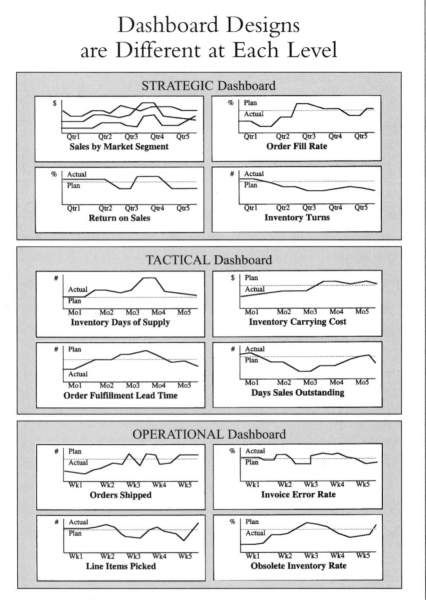

Dashboard Designs are Different at Each Level

People at different levels in an organization need to design their dashboard displays so that they get quick and easy access to the data they need to do their jobs and monitor their progress.

that can see their markets change and adjust and follow those markets most efficiently are the ones that will stay in business. Companies that do not notice problems soon enough or that do not see how their markets change are the ones that will get into trouble. See Exhibit 5.2.

Markets Migrate from One Quadrant to Another

Markets migrate from one quadrant to another during the course of their lifecycle. Over time, market forces are always pushing a market toward an equilibrium where supply meets demand. At the same time, other forces also influence a market so it fluctuates back and forth around the equilibrium point. At times demand outstrips supply and at other times there is more supply than there is demand.

Companies in the supply chains that supply a market must be able to adjust their operations over time as their markets migrate from one quadrant to another in order to remain competitive. For instance, in growth markets, supply chains that do the best are the ones that have the highest levels of customer service as measured by order fill rate and on-time delivery. All the companies in the supply chain must focus on delivering this performance in order to succeed.

As a growth market moves on to a steady market, the most profitable companies will be those that are able to maintain high levels of existing customer service and also broaden the scope of their customer services. In addition, profitable companies will be the ones that achieve the best levels of internal efficiency. They can no longer focus only on customer service.

As steady markets become mature markets, the supply chains that serve them must again develop their performance in another category. Mature markets require companies to develop the capabilities needed to accommodate high levels of demand flexibility. Then in the midst of mature markets, new developing markets can appear and the ability to create new products and bring them to market becomes critical.

Adaptability itself is now as important to survival and success as the four performance categories. Market evolution is now often measured in years and sometimes in months. Gone are the days when markets changed more slowly over decades. No company has the luxury of being able to focus on optimizing any single mix of performance capabilities over the long term.

A company may become very skilled at internal efficiency and customer service as called for in a steady market. The company needs to remember though that its markets will change. The company will have to add skills in the area of demand flexibility as some of its markets mature. The company may even need to de-emphasize some of its internal efficiency policies in order to emphasize its performance in product development so that it can participate in a promising developing market. The key here is that a company needs to know when to shift its emphasis from one mix of performance categories to another.

A ship at sea needs to watch the wind and the waves and respond appropriately when the weather changes. So too must a company watch the supply and demand situation in its markets and respond appropriately when one of its markets enters a new quadrant. If the collection and display of market and company performance data alerts a company to respond sooner to a market change than its competitors, then the company has indeed developed an important tool for its success and survival. See Exhibit 5.3.

Sharing Data Across the Supply Chain

As markets migrate from one quadrant to another, there are great demands placed on the supply chains that support them. In fact, it is sometimes the operation of the supply chain itself that can push a market from one quadrant to another. A case in point is illustrated by the beer game simulation described in Chapter 3. This simulation shows how a slight change in

EXHIBIT 5.3

Market Conditions Shift Over Time

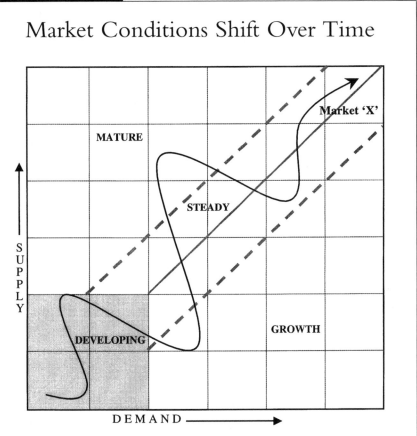

A market (call it Market 'X') follows a lifecycle. It develops and then it goes on to become a growth market which leads to a steady market and then a mature market and so on. Over time the forces of supply and demand are always pushing the market toward a steady state where supply and demand are equal yet at the same time other forces disrupt this balance.

The supply chains that support Market 'X' need to be able to provide first one kind of performance and then another as the market moves through its lifecycle. The companies that are most successful in supplying this market are those that can adapt their performance appropriately to follow the market as it changes.

demand by the end customer or the market can cause wildly escalating product demand forecasts to be sent to companies further down the supply chain. This "bullwhip" effect results in the production of large quantities of inventory which can then outstrip the real demand in the market. This event becomes the event that pushes a market out of the steady quadrant and into the mature quadrant. As excess inventory gets used up, it gradually brings the market back into the steady quadrant.

The cure for the bullwhip effect is better sharing of data among all the companies in a supply chain. Companies need to work through their concerns about sharing data that many of them might consider confidential. There are serious questions to be answered. What data is it reasonable to share? How can privacy of critical data be maintained? What are the benefits of sharing data and how can they be quantified?

Hau Lee is a professor at Stanford University's business school and director of the Stanford Global Supply Chain Management Forum. He envisions the supply chain as an "intricate network of suppliers, distributors and customers who share carefully managed information about demand, decisions and performance, and who recognize that success for one part of the supply chain means success for all."

If each company had demand information from the other companies in its supply chain, it would help everyone to make the best decisions about how much manufacturing capacity to build and how much inventory to hold. Companies need to see demand information from their immediate customers and also from the end customers that the supply chain ultimately supports.

In addition to sharing demand data across the supply chain, companies need to share decisions they make that have supply chain implications. A company could be unaware of decisions made by one of its customers or one of its customer's customers that will have a big impact on product demand. For instance, a chain of retail stores may decide to run a special promotion on a certain group of products. An analysis of past seasonal sales data would not predict the spike in demand that will result from running this promotion. So if the retail store chain does not share this decision with its suppliers, there is a very good chance they will be caught short and not be able to deliver enough product to support the promotion.

It is also important for companies to let each other know how well they are doing in the performance of their supply chain activities. These metrics can then be combined to provide a holistic picture of the performance of the entire supply chain. When each company in a supply chain sees how the supply chain is working overall, then each company can make better individual decisions about where performance improvements are needed.

At present, companies are most likely to share demand information with each other. There is already a lot of precedent for doing this. However, companies are much less likely to share their decisions or performance metrics because they are afraid that if this information gets out, it could wind up in the hands of their competitors and be used against them. The need for sharing this information continues to grow though. Customers continue to demand more and more from their supply chains. In an interview with *CIO Magazine* for an article titled "The Cost of Secrecy," professor Hau Lee said, "If you are late because your distributor is late, your customers will go to a competitor whose distributor isn't late. That is more than a company-to-company competition. We're going to see more supply-chain-to-supply-chain competition."

Companies that can work together to create efficient supply chains are going to be the ones that do the best over the long term. Companies that can figure out how to share data effectively will be the ones to create the most competitive supply chains. Customers are attracted to efficient supply chains and they gain market share at the expense of less efficient supply chains. See Exhibit 5.4.

EXHIBIT 5.4

Benefits of Data Sharing Across the Entire Supply Chain

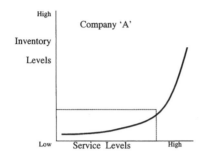

An individual company can achieve high levels of customer service to its customer. However, this customer may not be the end use customer that the supply chain ultimately serves, in which case, the company may find that its success is short lived.

Company 'A' may be part of a supply chain (Supply Chain 'Y') that actually maintains higher levels of inventory across the entire supply chain to deliver the required level of customer service. A competing supply chain that does not maintain as much inventory will be more profitable and can take more market share.

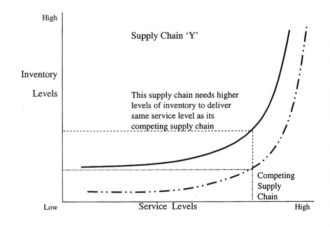

Whole supply chains can become more efficient if they are able to better coordinate their operations. As supply and demand conditions change, coordination of inventory levels is critical to business success.

EXECUTIVE INSIGHT

Business realities do not always support the sharing of data among supply chain partners. Concerns about privacy and competitive advantage often lead companies not to share data such as sales and demand forecasts.

Jim Alexy is the CEO of Network Services Company, a multi-billion dollar distribution organization. Prior to coming to Network Services he held senior management positions at several of the manufacturers whose products Network Services sells. He can speak from the perspective of both the manufacturer and the distributor.

When asked about his experience in sharing data with other companies in a supply chain, he thought for a moment and then responded, "In a perfect world, yes it's a great idea...but if you do share the data, it's only a matter of time before some company turns it against you. Each company has its own quarterly management incentive plans and people will do what they need to do to meet their numbers."

Companies do share data about things such as product demand and inventory levels. The problem is that companies often modify this data to their own advantage. Customers often inflate their demand numbers in order to ensure that they will get the amount of product they think they will really need. Jim said, "Most manufacturers have some sort of productivity targets they need to hit. When they look at the demand data they get from customers it is so inaccurate that if they responded to all the fluctuations, their production costs would go up and they still wouldn't be producing the right items anyway."

So companies take the data that others share with them and run their own projections. "When I was CEO at Sweetheart Cups," said Jim, "there was a guy who worked for me who built these great demand forecast models. He collected all the data and factored in historical trends and ran the model. Then he looked at the results and tweaked them in places where he had a strong hunch or some special information. And then after all of that, his forecasts still weren't as accurate as they could be because one of our major customers like McDonald's wouldn't tell us about a big promotion they were planning to run and we'd be caught short in 12 ounce cups or something. They didn't always tell us because they didn't want word to get out and then have a competitor take action to counter their promotion." Because of the "tweaking" that companies do, the data can get pretty distorted at times. And since demand data needs to be much more accurate and believable before a company is going to accept it at face value, the tweaking will continue.

In spite of these issues, data sharing has enabled some major supply chain improvements. "I think there has been a lot of inventory taken out of the system," said Jim. "Just-in-time inventory has resulted in major savings for everyone." Just-in-time inventory is often implemented through a technique called vendor managed inventory or VMI. Using this technique, the suppliers of products monitor inventory levels of their products within the companies that they sell to. Their customers share inventory usage data and sales numbers and the supplier keeps the inventory stocked at the right levels.

Companies are always weighing the costs and benefits of sharing data and working together using techniques like VMI. "The whole concept of VMI is a very powerful concept. So why don't I just pick a small group of key suppliers and have them manage all my inventory for me? Well, the other side of that question is why do I want to be in bed with just a few suppliers? They can arbitrarily change pricing, or have strikes or other production problems."

It is very hard for companies to develop the level of credibility and trust needed to establish tight working relationships. In the meantime, companies still benefit from developing the skill sets and tools that allow them to analyze data and make decisions. "There is too much

Chapter Summary

A useful model of markets can be constructed using the basic components of supply and demand. Using these two components results in a model that defines four market quadrants:

1. DEVELOPING—New markets and new products where both supply and demand are low and uncertain

2. GROWTH—Markets where demand is higher than supply and supply is uncertain

3. STEADY—Established markets where supply is high and demand is high and both are stable and predictable

4. MATURE—Markets where supply exceeds demand and where demand can be unpredictable

The markets in each quadrant have a unique set of performance requirements that they place on their supply chains. Developing markets require performance in the areas of customer service and product development. Growth markets demand customer service above all else. Steady markets call for customer service and for internal efficiency, and mature markets require customer service, internal efficiency, and demand flexibility. In order to succeed, companies and supply chains must excel in the performance areas that are required by the markets they serve.

Customer service performance is measured by metrics such as order and line item fill rate, on-time delivery, and item return rates. Internal efficiency refers to the ability of a company or supply chain to use its assets as profitably as possible. Popular measures of internal efficiency are metrics such as inventory value, inventory turns, and return on sales. Demand flexibility describes the ability of a company or supply chain to be responsive to sudden market demands for greatly increased quantities of product or for additional products outside the normal bundle of products provided. Product development measures an organization's ability to design, build, and deliver new products to serve their markets as those markets evolve over time. Performance in this area is most important in developing markets.

CHAPTER 6

Defining Supply Chain Opportunities

After reading this chapter you will be able to

- Apply the market analysis framework to define the type of markets your company serves and identify the performance capabilities most valuable to those markets

- Define performance targets for your company to succeed in the markets you serve—the goal

- Create a strategy and define the objectives needed to reach the goal

- Estimate the budget needed for this effort and calculate the return on investment (ROI)

- Create the high-level project plan that will guide the effort

N ow that conscious design and real-time management of a company's supply chain is possible, how does a company use this ability to its competitive advantage? A well designed and managed supply chain will enable a company to offer high levels of customer service and at the same time hold its inventories and cost of sales to levels lower than its competitors. This chapter will lay out a process to use for defining the supply chain management opportunities available to a company.

The Supply Chain as a Competitive Advantage

As companies such as Wal-Mart and Dell Computer have so clearly shown, if a company can design and build a supply chain that is responsive to market demands, it can grow from a small company to become a major player. Efficient supply chain operations are central to being able to satisfy market demands and to do so in a way that is profitable. Where once markets were shaped by the availability of product, now they are shaped by the evolving demands (some might say whims) of the end use customers. Availability of most products is now taken for granted. So in addition to the product itself, the market has a host of other requirements in the areas of customer service, demand flexibility, and product development. A company needs to understand where it fits in the supply chains of the markets it serves. Then it needs to decide which activities it will focus on to deliver value.

Supply chains that deliver the best value to their end use customers generate a strong demand for products and services. They are good places for producers, logistics providers, distributors, and retailers to do business. The efficiency of the entire supply chain greatly affects each company's ability to prosper, so standards of performance evolve in these supply chains over time. New companies cannot enter unless they can meet these standards. What this means is that companies who are good at their core supply chain operations work together in self-selecting supply chains to deliver the greatest value to the end use customer.

It also means that there is great profit potential to be had for companies in a supply chain who learn to cooperate to generate efficiencies and cost savings for all. Skilled companies in specific markets that learn to work together to achieve new levels of efficiency and cost savings will create supply chains that grow faster than other supply chains in their markets.

We may even begin to look at a market in terms of the competing supply chains that support it instead of just the competing supplier

Companies that work together in supply chains conduct an ongoing discussion about the value perceived and paid for between supply chain partners. The balance of power in the supply chain is always being explored.

Walt Dethlefsen is the executive vice president of Network Services Company. Network Services is a distribution organization that handles a bundle of products that includes printing paper and paper products, food service disposables, and janitorial supplies. Network Services participates in the supply chains of customers such as Starbucks, Baskin-Robbins, 24 Hour Fitness Clubs, and Premier Health Care. The company distributes the products of manufacturers such as Georgia-Pacific, Kimberly Clark, Johnson Wax, 3M, and Rubbermaid.

One of Walt's main activities is to manage the relationships that Network Services has with its suppliers. His work gives him a first-hand view on a weekly basis of what it means to work in evolving supply chains with demanding customers and manufacturers. "Big manufacturers used to have the most power but that is shifting towards the big customer. Big customers now go directly to the manufacturers whose products they want to negotiate prices on and then they go to the distributor and negotiate the cost for product delivery.

"The distributor often has the least power now. For years the distributor was in the middle and could negotiate with both sides—the customer on one hand and the manufacturer on the other. There were distributors who did a very good job negotiating with one or the other and sometimes both parties." Customers these days have many choices in what they buy and are very successful in driving down prices. Manufacturers are also able to use many different channels to market so they demand greater and greater performance from the distributors they work with.

"The only distributors who are able to defy the price squeeze and maintain reasonable margins are the ones who are able to create a brand. Typically they recreate their whole company into a brand. The brand stands for all the products they sell plus everything else that they provide for the customer. When the customer buys from them they know that trucks will show up at the right time with the right stuff, that they will get quality products and top notch customer service, all at a fair acquisition cost."

The power of the distributor in a supply chain depends very much on the type of manufacturers that they work with. "I would say we work with three kinds of manufacturers," says Walt. The first kind is the brand name manufacturer who has a retail consumer side of their company as well as a business-to-business side. "What they mostly expect from the distributor is logistics and customer support in the field."

The second kind of manufacturer focuses mainly on the business-to-business market and views the distributor as their customer. "They are generally selective and will only sell to distribution that gives them a lot of participation. They typically limit the number of distributors in a market if they are satisfied with the penetration they provide."

In the third group of manufacturers are companies who are basically converters or smaller manufacturers. Converters take a finished product from another manufacturer and further customize it. For instance, they may buy bulk rolls of towel and tissue grade paper and cut it to customer specifications. Also in this group are small specialty manufacturers of product lines that have little brand recognition. "These companies are the ones who are most dependent on the distributor to get their product to market. They have small sales forces and rely on distributors to develop the end use market for their products. They produce products with little known brand names and typically they lead with price."

companies within the market. Just as we now rate individual companies by their profitability and customer service levels, we may begin to measure entire supply chains on their overall performance in these areas.

Identify the Business Opportunity and Define the Goal

Supply chain opportunities generally come in one of two categories. The first category is to fix or improve something already in place. The second category is to build something new. In both categories you have to first define the goal and then set about to accomplish that goal. Depending on which type of opportunity you are pursuing, the way to accomplish the goal will be different.

If you are pursuing an opportunity that is in the "fix or improve something already existing" category, then use Mr. Goldratt's theory of constraints as your guidelines for taking action. These guidelines are summarized in an executive insight section in Chapter 3. If you are going after an opportunity in the "build something new" category, then use the process outlined in this chapter.

New markets emerge, existing markets evolve, and mature markets fade away. A market creates a demand for a bundle of products and services to support it. Over the life span of a market its supply chain evolves in response to the forces of supply and demand. Companies that supply a market must evolve along with the demands of that market. What are the markets your company serves and who are the end use customers in these markets? Who are the producers in these markets? Who are the distributors, the logistics providers, and the retailers? What are the products and services demanded by this market?

What is the supply and demand situation in the markets you serve? The supply chain opportunities available to a company depend on which quadrants the markets it serves are in. Use the market analysis framework to determine which market quadrants your company deals with. Which quadrants are your markets in today? Which quadrants do you think they will be in two years from now? Compare your organization against competing organizations in your markets. Identify whether you lead, equal, or lag your competitors in the areas of:

- Customer Service
- Internal Efficiency
- Demand Flexibility
- Product Development

Each market is best served by some combination of performance in these four areas. Define whether your company needs to lead, equal, or even excel in each of these areas. Identify the position your company needs to take in the four areas to best align itself with the demands of the markets it serves.

As discussed in Chapter 4, a company must lead in flexibility if its target markets are in quadrant three, and it must lead in internal efficiency if its markets are in quadrant four. A company must excel in product development if its markets are in quadrant one and companies must meet high customer service standards in all market quadrants. Set the performance targets needed to achieve this market alignment. These performance targets define the goal. They become the measures of success.

Create the Strategy

Once a business goal is defined and the performance targets are set, the next step is to create a strategy to accomplish this. Strategy can be defined as simply, "the use of means to achieve ends." In other words, a strategy uses the business operations (means) of an organization to achieve its goals (ends).

To define the strategy, begin by looking at the supply chain operations that are performed in your company. Achieving the performance targets that have been set will require improvements in one or more of the four categories of business operations that are used to manage the supply chain:

- Plan
- Source
- Make
- Deliver

Use Brainstorming to Generate Ideas

Brainstorm a large list of improvement ideas for the operations under each of the four categories. Ask the question, " What seems impossible to do, but if it could be done, would dramatically change the way we do business?" Look for ways to change the business landscape—ways to give your organization a significant competitive advantage by doing something new and different. Where no new ideas are found, look for ways to significantly improve existing operations to get greater performance and better cost savings. Better efficiencies in existing operations will rarely provide huge business wins but they help ensure the company's survival.

Take the time to work up a large list of ideas. These ideas are the raw material from which the business strategy will emerge. When a sufficiently large body of ideas has been generated, review the lists and select three to six or so of the ideas that seem to have the most impact. These are ideas that will deliver improvements in multiple operations or performance categories. They are also ideas that promise the greatest payback and have the highest likelihood of success. These are the ideas that now need to get further attention. They will be the foundation upon which the strategy is based. See Exhibit 6.1.

EXHIBIT 6.1

Improve Selected Business Operations to Meet Performance Targets

BUSINESS OPERATIONS	PERFORMANCE CATEGORIES	CUSTOMER SERVICE As measured by: Fill Rate; On-Time Delivery; Product Returns	INTERNAL EFFICIENCY As measured by: Inventory Turns; Return on Sales; Cash-to-Cash	DEMAND FLEXIBILITY As measured by: Cycle Times; Upside Flex; Outside Flex	PRODUCT DEVELOPMENT As measured by: New Prod Sales; % Revenue; Cycle Time
P L A N	Demand Forecast	X	X	X	
	Product Pricing	X	X		
	Inventory Management	X	X	X	
S O U R C E	Procurement		X	X	
	Credit & Collections	X	X		
M A K E	Product Design	X			X
	Production Scheduling		X	X	
	Facility Management	X	X		
D E L I V E R	Order Management	X	X		X
	Delivery Scheduling	X	X		

Network Services set a goal and performance targets that called for improvements in the categories of customer service and demand flexibility. To excel in these two categories, Network Services Co. had earlier made major improvements in its credit and collections operations. Next, it decided to improve its demand forecasting, product pricing, and order management operations.

Examine this handful of most promising ideas that have been selected. How will these ideas play out over the next few years? How do these ideas work together to form a big picture sequence of events that will take the organization from where it presently is to where it wants to go—the accomplishment of its business goals? What things have to be done, what new operating procedures and information systems need to be created in order to carry out these ideas? What are the best guesses as to the time it will take to create these new operating procedures and systems?

Look to see how these ideas relate to each other. Does the implementation of one idea build upon the implementation of a previous idea? What sequence should be followed in the implementation of these ideas? What kind of changes in operations, technology, and staffing are called for to implement each idea and how can these changes be done in a manageable way? How can the implementation of these ideas be broken up into phases that can each be completed in three to nine months? A phase needs to create deliverables that provide value in their own right and that can be put to use as soon as the phase is completed. See Exhibit 6.2.

It is important to both see the big picture that stretches over a period of several years and also to segment this big picture into smaller phases. This way the company is able to begin receiving tangible benefits from its work in a relatively short period of time. It can also respond to new developments in the business environment in a timely manner by adjusting its strategy as necessary as it completes each phase. There is a saying that sums up this approach very nicely: "Think big, start small, and deliver quickly."

Create a Conceptual System Design

The strategy to achieve the business goals is expressed in the conceptual design. The conceptual design is the high-level outline of a system or a set of systems. Generate several different conceptual designs for systems

EXHIBIT 6.2

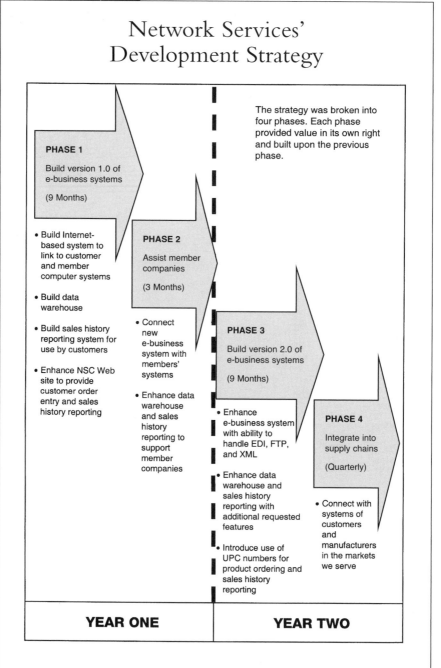

Network Services'
Development Strategy

The strategy was broken into four phases. Each phase provided value in its own right and built upon the previous phase.

PHASE 1

Build version 1.0 of e-business systems

(9 Months)

- Build Internet-based system to link to customer and member computer systems

- Build data warehouse

- Build sales history reporting system for use by customers

- Enhance NSC Web site to provide customer order entry and sales history reporting

PHASE 2

Assist member companies

(3 Months)

- Connect new e-business system with members' systems

- Enhance data warehouse and sales history reporting to support member companies

PHASE 3

Build version 2.0 of e-business systems

(9 Months)

- Enhance e-business system with ability to handle EDI, FTP, and XML

- Enhance data warehouse and sales history reporting with additional requested features

- Introduce use of UPC numbers for product ordering and sales history reporting

PHASE 4

Integrate into supply chains

(Quarterly)

- Connect with systems of customers and manufacturers in the markets we serve

YEAR ONE | **YEAR TWO**

that will meet the desired performance criteria. Approach the conceptual design first from the perspective of the business processes that are supported. Sketch out the different operations that are performed and note the kind of information that is required by and created by each operation.

Then add further definition to these process flows by specifying the data flows into and out of each operation. For each operation, estimate the volume and frequency of the data flows and also the source and destination of each data flow. In addition, for each operation, define the types of people (if any) who will perform this work. How many people will there be? What are the skill levels of the different types of people? This kind of business process diagram is illustrated in Exhibit 6.3.

Next, decide which operation will be automated, which will be manual, and which will be part automated and part manual. As a rule, people will like systems that automate the rote and repetitive tasks and empower them to do the problem-solving and decision-making tasks more effectively. People really are the most valuable resource of any company, so design systems that make maximum use of their skills. Technology's role is to support the people who use it, not the other way around.

Evaluate the existing computer system's infrastructure in place in your organization. Look for ways to build on that infrastructure. The most cost effective systems are those that deliver valuable new capabilities to an organization quickly and with a minimum of effort.

Select the simplest combinations of technology and business processes that will meet the specified performance criteria. Balance the need for simplicity with the ability to increase the capacity of the system to handle greater volumes of data and to add new functionality as the business operations grow in volume. And remember that markets move over time from one quadrant to another so build a supply chain infrastructure that is flexible enough to change with the needs of the markets your

EXHIBIT 6.3

Diagram of the Business Process Flows

Network Services: E-Business Process Flows

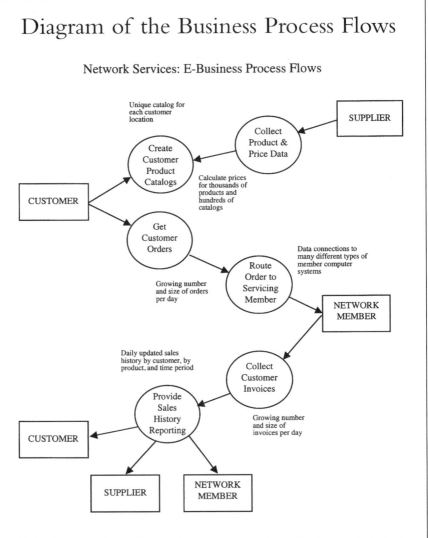

This diagram shows the business process flows that were included in the design of the first version of the Network Services e-business system.

company serves. Do not design a system that locks the company into one way of operating and that is not capable of evolving to support new operations.

Create high level schematic diagrams to illustrate each conceptual system design. In these diagrams use simple shapes like cubes and cylinders and spheres to represent different components of the design. Connect these shapes with lines and arrows to show the direction of data flow and activity. Do not get too technical or detailed in these diagrams. Their purpose is to quickly communicate the basic structure of the proposed designs.

These schematic diagrams are invaluable in communicating the features of the different designs to a wide audience of people. Reviews and comments should be sought from people who will use the new system, people who will pay for it, and people who will build it. Thoughtful input from a wide audience of people is very helpful in selecting the best design and then in adjusting that design to increase the likelihood that it will succeed.

Strategic Guidelines for Designing Systems

Designing supply chain systems or any other kind of system can quickly become a very complex undertaking. The business manager can come to feel overwhelmed by the possible choices and be tempted to leave this activity to the technical experts. Do not give in to this temptation. Business management must remain actively involved with the technical people in creating the conceptual design for the system. It is in this activity that the business manager can exercise very effective control over the strategy that the company will take to accomplish its goal. This activity cannot be left entirely to technical people because they usually do not have the depth of business knowledge that is needed to make the best decisions.

The best approach is for business and technical people to work together and generate a number of possible conceptual designs. Evaluate the goodness of each conceptual design by applying the seven guidelines for the design of new systems. These guidelines provide a basis to compare different designs and to select the conceptual design that has the best chance of success. A design that respects all seven of these guidelines is the best. It may still be a workable design if one or two of these guidelines are violated (as long as it is not the first of the seven guidelines shown below). If guidelines are violated, there need to be very good reasons for doing so and specific compensations made to cover those violations. If three or more guidelines are broken, then the conceptual design is seriously flawed and it is very unlikely that the design can be successfully built.

The seven system design guidelines are:

1. *Closely align system designs with the business goals and performance targets they are intended to accomplish.* For any systems development project to be a success it must directly support the organization to achieve one or more of its goals. No new system can be effective until you have first identified or created the business opportunity that will make the system worth building and no new system will bring any sustained benefit to your company unless it supports the efficient exploitation of the business opportunity it was built to address.

2. *Use systems to change the competitive landscape.* Ask yourself what seems impossible to do today, but if it could be done, would fundamentally change what your company does in a positive way. Put yourself in your customers' shoes. In the words of the Nordstrom's motto, think of what would "surprise and delight" your customers. Look for opportunities to create a transforma-

tion or value shift in your market. Find ways to do things that provide dramatic cost savings or productivity increases. Place yourself in your competitor's shoes and think of what course you could take that would be the least likely to be foreseen or quickly countered or copied. As long as you are able to do something of value that your competitors cannot, you have an advantage. If you are going to take bigger risks and incur larger costs to develop a system, then make sure it is a system that will change the competitive landscape. This is the kind of system that can deliver benefits that might justify bigger risks and costs.

3. *Leverage the strengths of existing systems infrastructure.* When existing systems have proven over time to be stable and responsive, find ways to incorporate them into the design of new systems. The purpose of strategy is to best use the means available to the organization to accomplish its goal. The design of a system is the embodiment of the strategy being used. Build new systems on the strengths of older systems. That is what nature does in the evolutionary process. New systems provide value only insofar as they provide new business capabilities. Time spent replacing old systems with new systems that do essentially the same things will not, as a general rule, provide enough value to justify the cost.

4. *Use the simplest possible combination of technology and business procedures to achieve the maximum number of performance targets.* A simple mix of technology and process that can achieve several different performance targets increases the probability that at least some performance targets can actually be achieved. This is because simple combinations of technology and business process reduce the complexity and the risk associated with the systems. Using a different combination of technology and business process

to achieve each different performance target multiplies the cost and the complexity of the entire undertaking and reduces the overall probability of success.

5. *Structure the design so as to provide flexibility in the development sequence used to create the system.* Break the system design into separate components or objectives and as much as possible, run the work on individual objectives in parallel. Try not to make the achievement of one objective dependent on the prior achievement of another objective. In this way, delays in the work toward one objective will not impact the progress toward other objectives. Use people on the project who have skills that can be used to achieve a variety of different objectives. If you use the same technology to achieve several different objectives, it is much easier to shift people from one objective to another as needed because the skill sets used are the same. Your project plan should foresee and provide for an alternative plan in case of failure or delays in achieving objectives as scheduled. The design of the system you are building should allow you to cut some system features if needed and yet still be able to deliver solid value to the business.

6. *Do not try to build a system whose complexity exceeds the organization's capabilities.* The beginning of wisdom is a sense of what is possible so don't bite off more than you can chew. When defining business goals and the systems to reach those goals, aim for things that are within your reach. Set challenging goals but not hopeless goals. The people in your organization need to have confidence in themselves in order to rise to a challenge. Avoid exhausting their confidence in vain efforts to reach unrealistic goals.

7. *Do not renew a project using the same people or the same system design after it has once failed.* A mere reinforcement of effort or just trying harder is not a sufficient enough change to ensure the success of a project after it has once failed. People are probably demoralized after the first failure and will not rise to the challenge of doing the work again unless there are meaningful changes in the project approach. The new approach must clearly reflect what was learned from the previous failure and offer a better way to achieve the business goal and performance targets.

TIPS & TECHNIQUES

Strategic System Design Guidelines

The seven system design guidelines are:

❶ Closely align system designs with the business goals and performance targets they are intended to accomplish.

❷ Use systems to change the competitive landscape.

❸ Leverage the strengths of existing systems infrastructure.

❹ Use the simplest possible combination of technology and business procedures to achieve the maximum number of performance targets.

❺ Structure the design so as to provide flexibility in the development sequence used to create the system.

❻ Do not try to build a system whose complexity exceeds the organization's capabilities.

❼ Do not renew a project using the same people or the same system design after it has once failed.

IN THE REAL WORLD

Network Services applied the strategic guidelines for designing systems to create a conceptual design for its e-business systems infrastructure.

Network Services selected a conceptual design for its e-business systems infrastructure that would best enable it to meet its performance targets. This design was presented to an audience that ranged from the board of directors to senior management to the people who would build the systems infrastructure and the people who would use the systems. Feedback from all these people helped to finalize the design. The schematic diagram for this conceptual design is shown in Exhibit 6.4.

The systems infrastructure is composed of four main components that work together to provide a flexible and cost effective infrastructure that can change as business conditions evolve and can handle greater and greater volumes of data as business operations grow. The four main components are:

❶ *The Extranet*—A high-speed, Internet-based network to provide all member companies with a secure environment in which to exchange information and work together to serve national accounts.

❷ *Web-Based E-Commerce Systems*—A suite of systems accessed via the Network Services web site. A packaged system from an application service provider (ASP) named Tibersoft is used to provide order entry, inventory, and order status. Network Services provides the sales history reporting system. This suite of e-commerce systems is also available to member companies to serve their local customers.

❸ *NSC Data Warehouse*—A collection of databases to support the web-based e-commerce operations and internal NSC operations such as proposal development, price file maintenance, account book creation, and sales reporting.

IN THE REAL WORLD (CONTINUED)

④ Data Delivery System (NetLink-NSC™)—A two-way, Internet-based data transfer system to allow each member company's internal systems to read and write data in a common format to support delivery of seamless and consistent national account service. This component incorporated and reused software from an earlier system that provided for receipt and error checking of invoice data from member companies.

EXHIBIT 6.4

Conceptual Design for E–Business Systems Infrastructure

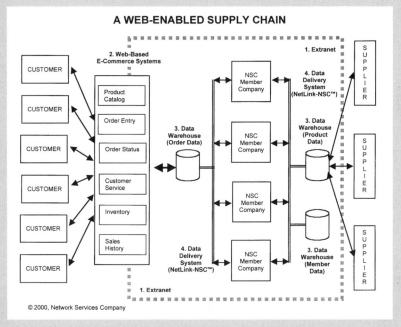

A WEB-ENABLED SUPPLY CHAIN

© 2000, Network Services Company

The greatest value for the company lay in the construction of the data warehouse to house the databases and in building the data delivery system called "NetLink-NSC™." Those components working together would best meet the performance criteria defined by the company. In order to meet the financial performance criteria and reduce project risk, Network Services decided to lease the use of an existing Web-based product catalog and order entry system instead of building its own.

Define Project Objectives

When you look at a schematic diagram that illustrates a conceptual design, the system is shown as a set of high-level components. Defining these high-level components is a somewhat subjective process since there is a range of possible ways to design a system—some better than others. The better designs will define high-level components that are highly cohesive in the functions they perform. This means that each component performs a set of tasks that are all closely related to a single and well-defined activity. For instance, a highly cohesive component in a conceptual design could be an order entry system. This component does all the things that need to be done for a customer to enter an order and that is all it does.

A component that is not cohesive would be a component that did order entry and also managed a database of sales information and also routed orders to different business locations. Showing all those activities as one component in a schematic design does not provide enough definition of the design to enable people to evaluate it effectively. This component should be broken down into three separate components— one for order entry, one for database management, and one for data transmission.

The building of each of these high-level components defines a set of specific, measurable activities or objectives that need to be achieved in order to create the system. There will tend to be somewhere between three to nine high-level components and all other components will resolve into sub-components of these high-level components. Why only three to nine high-level components? Because most of us are just regular folks and we cannot comprehend at a glance or remember more than seven (plus or minus two) things at a time. A clear and simple system design goes a long way toward insuring the success of the project because the people involved with it can understand it.

If a conceptual design is produced that is so complex only a genius can understand it, then the conceptual design is useless. People will not be able to use it to effectively guide their work in the detailed design and building of the system. Without a clear conceptual design, the people involved with building, using, and paying for the system will all have different ideas about what the company is trying to accomplish. People working on the different parts of the system will find it increasingly difficult to coordinate their actions with each other. The level of tension and misunderstanding and arguing will rise higher and higher as the work continues.

The development of each component in the conceptual system design becomes an objective in the project to build the system. Similar to the way that a long-term strategy is broken down into self-sufficient phases that each provide value in their own right, the building of a new system should be broken down into a set of objectives that each provide value in their own right. An objective should not be just an intermediate step along the way that depends on the completion of some future step to be of value. Objectives should each be achievable in three to nine months (or less). Look for objectives that can be achieved quickly. These will begin providing value and repaying the cost of the project before it is even entirely finished. Once achieved, an objective should become a base from which other objectives can be achieved.

Also be careful not to define objectives that lock the project into some rigid sequence of development activities. The world rarely goes according to plan, so the plan must be flexible in order to adapt as reality unfolds. Begin work on as many objectives as possible at the same time (in parallel). As much as possible, make the tasks needed to achieve each objective independent of the tasks needed to achieve the other objectives. This provides maximum flexibility, so that if one objective is delayed, it will not also delay the completion of other objectives being done in parallel. Resources can then be shifted from one objective to another as needed to respond to situations that arise.

Create an Initial Project Plan and Budget

It is always a challenge to create a project plan early in the project when there are so many things that are not entirely known. There will be much agonizing and grumbling about the plan. People will feel that they are being asked to commit to something that they know very little about and that whatever they say will come back to haunt them. In an attempt to give themselves as much wiggle room as possible, some people will create plans that are so high level and vague that they are little more than smoke screens. Other people will plunge into the task with determination and produce a plan showing minute detail about things that can hardly be defined yet. These plans are little more than wishful thinking about a future that will probably be nothing like what is shown.

So what is to be done? Let's start with a definition. Simply stated, a plan is a sequence of non-repetitive tasks that lead to the achievement of one or more predefined objectives that do not yet exist. A plan should not be confused with an operating schedule, which is a repetitive sequence of tasks that perpetuate an already existing state of affairs. This means that the plan should focus on laying out the tasks that need to be performed to achieve each objective that was identified in the conceptual system design. Do not clutter up the project plan with repetitive tasks that are related to ongoing administrative or business operations.

Create a section of the overall project plan for each objective. In the section of the plan for each objective, list the major tasks needed to achieve that objective. There will be tasks related to designing and then building the deliverables necessary for each objective. Show the dependencies between the tasks related to an objective and show the dependencies between the objectives.

When estimating how long each task will take, remember the old saying that "any job will expand to fill the time available." Use a technique called "time boxing" to define the time limits for each task. This technique calls for a trade-off between the work involved in carrying out a task and the time that is available. Realistic and adequate time periods must be assigned to each task but then it is up to the people doing the work to tailor the job to fit the time that is allocated. When setting these time boxes, get input from the people who will be asked to do the work. In a good plan the time boxes for each task are aggressive and they require people to work hard and stay focused, but they should not be so aggressive as to make people feel they have no chance of getting the work done.

A useful way to think about the work on a project and the corresponding time boxes is to divide time spent on a project into three main steps and assign an overall time box to each of the main steps. Then within each step, subdivide the time available to accommodate the tasks that are involved. The three steps and their durations are:

1. Define what is going to be done—the goal and the objectives. (2–6 weeks)
2. Design how that will be done—the detailed specifications. (1–3 months)
3. Build what is specified. (2–6 months)

For each objective set a time box for the design step and the build step. Don't worry about the define step—that is what you are doing right now and showing it on the plan is not necessary. Look at the tasks that are required to achieve each objective. For example, let's say that Objective A has a one-month time box for design and a two-month time box for build. Decide which tasks fall into the design step and which tasks are in the build step. Allocate the time available in design among the tasks involved and do the same for the tasks in the build step.

EXHIBIT 6.5

How to Create an Initial Project Plan

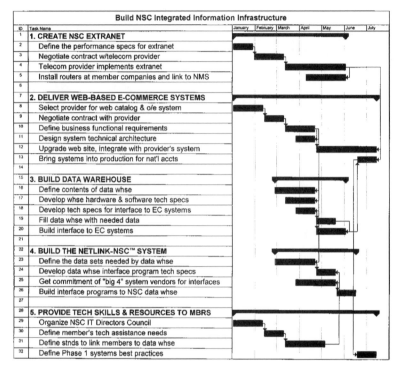

ID	Task Name	January	February	March	April	May	June	July
	Build NSC Integrated Information Infrastructure							
1	**1. CREATE NSC EXTRANET**							
2	Define the performance specs for extranet							
3	Negotiate contract w/telecom provider							
4	Telecom provider implements extranet							
5	Install routers at member companies and link to NMS							
6								
7	**2. DELIVER WEB-BASED E-COMMERCE SYSTEMS**							
8	Select provider for web catalog & o/e system							
9	Negotiate contract with provider							
10	Define business functional requirements							
11	Design system technical architecture							
12	Upgrade web site, integrate with provider's system							
13	Bring systems into production for nat'l accts							
14								
15	**3. BUILD DATA WAREHOUSE**							
16	Define contents of data whse							
17	Develop whse hardware & software tech specs							
18	Develop tech specs for interface to EC systems							
19	Fill data whse with needed data							
20	Build interface to EC systems							
21								
22	**4. BUILD THE NETLINK-NSC™ SYSTEM**							
23	Define the data sets needed by data whse							
24	Develop data whse interface program tech specs							
25	Get commitment of "big 4" system vendors for interfaces							
26	Build interface programs to NSC data whse							
27								
28	**5. PROVIDE TECH SKILLS & RESOURCES TO MBRS**							
29	Organize NSC IT Directors Council							
30	Define member's tech assistance needs							
31	Define stnds to link members to data whse							
32	Define Phase 1 systems best practices							

The Network Services Co. e-business project objectives were defined by the conceptual system design. The conceptual design had four components:

1. The Extranet

2. Web-Based E-Commerce Systems

3. The Data Warehouse

4. The NetLink-NSC™ Data Delivery System

Thus, the creation of each of these four components became a project objective. There was also a fifth objective to address the strategy of providing technical skills and resources to member companies. This initial project plan laid out the time boxes for the effort needed to achieve each objective. These time boxes defined the amount of time available for each activity. Work was then tailored to fit the times available.

You have now subdivided the larger design and build time boxes for Objective A into smaller time boxes for the tasks that are involved.

Assigning time boxes is an iterative process. It involves adjusting both the time allocations and the scope of the work that will be done. It will probably take several passes through the plan before you have something that seems reasonable—something that is both aggressive and yet still doable. See Exhibit 6.5 for an example of an initial project plan.

Estimate the Project Budget and ROI

This is the step where you answer one of the most fundamental questions about the project—"Is this project worth doing?" Once a plan has been constructed, the budget can be created. Project plans and budgets are just two sides of the same coin. Plans show the time, people, and material needed to get things done and budgets show the cost of the people and material over the time frames involved. Although, in many cases, the cost and benefits related to a project cannot be defined with absolute certainty, it is still a valuable exercise to get as accurate an estimate as possible.

The value comes in two areas. The first is that this is an opportunity to create a consensus among the people who have to pay for the system. Everyone whose budget will be affected by the project should have an opportunity to review the costs and the benefits of the project. It is often hard to assign specific values to the benefits but it must be done. When in doubt, understate the benefits—just make sure that the benefit numbers are ones that people can understand and support. The sum of these benefit numbers is the value of the project and it is very important to have agreement on the value of a project.

The value of the project is the main reference point to keep in mind when evaluating the rest of the project. The value of the system is what tells you how much can be spent to build the system. If the costs

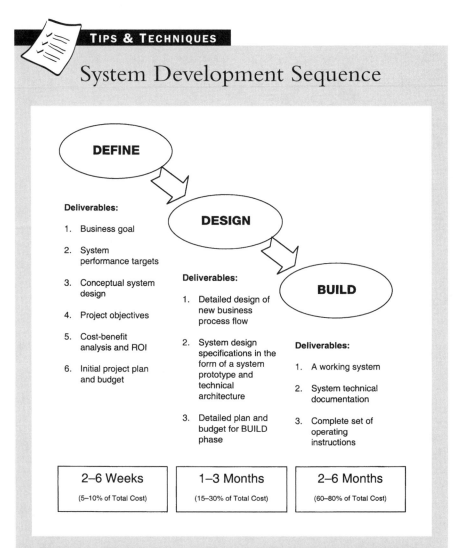

TIPS & TECHNIQUES

System Development Sequence

DEFINE

Deliverables:

1. Business goal

2. System performance targets

3. Conceptual system design

4. Project objectives

5. Cost-benefit analysis and ROI

6. Initial project plan and budget

DESIGN

Deliverables:

1. Detailed design of new business process flow

2. System design specifications in the form of a system prototype and technical architecture

3. Detailed plan and budget for BUILD phase

BUILD

Deliverables:

1. A working system

2. System technical documentation

3. Complete set of operating instructions

2–6 Weeks	1–3 Months	2–6 Months
(5–10% of Total Cost)	(15–30% of Total Cost)	(60–80% of Total Cost)

These three steps provide a useful way to think about the work that has to be done to create a new system. Under each step is shown the deliverables that need to be produced and estimating guidelines for how long each step should take to complete and how much of the total project budget should be spent on that step.

to develop a system add up to more than the benefits that will be produced, then there are two choices. Either find a less expensive way to produce those benefits or simply do not do the project. Businesses exist to make a profit and that is a discipline that all business people must live with.

Define the Specific Costs and Benefits

From a financial perspective, a system generates a stream of costs and benefits over the length of time in which it is built and used. As a rule, a system should pay for itself and return an appropriate profit within one to three years because after that time the system will usually need major enhancements or a complete reworking. Specific benefits need to be identified and estimates made of their dollar value. Measure system costs and benefits on a quarterly basis. Subtract costs from benefits to arrive at the quarterly cash flow generated by the system. Calculate the value of that cash flow using whatever method the financial decision-makers would like (net present value, internal rate of return, etc.). The higher the risk involved in building and operating the system, the higher the profit that the system should generate.

System Costs

In a system development project there are three types of costs:

1. Hardware and software costs for the hardware, software, and communication network components that need to be purchased from vendors for the new system design.

2. Development costs as estimated by the time and cost needed to achieve each project objective. Each task that is part of the work plan for an objective will require some number of people with certain skills for some period of time. Each task will also require certain technology and perhaps other expenses, such as travel, hotel rooms, and meals. Set a standard cost for each kind of person and

Cost/benefit analysis calls for finance executives to exercise judgment based on experience and industry norms.

Network Services' CFO, Bob Mitchum, uses some rules of thumb when he looks at a cost/benefit analysis. "First of all, I use a 12- to 18-month time frame for the analysis and I need to see an attractive payback in that time. If you accept a three- to five-year payback period you are probably using the analysis to justify what is really an emotional decision. Beyond 18 months the world changes in ways you cannot predict and I don't think you can effectively estimate numbers that far out."

Costs are usually easier to estimate than benefits. A realistic estimate of benefits is very important. "Look at the tangible benefits and try to assign some numbers over a period of time. Then look at other intangible benefits such as reputation and relationships with customers and suppliers. Look at employee productivity and leveraging their talents. Who are the stakeholders? What are the alternatives to doing the project and getting the same benefits?

"When I looked at the design and the cost benefit analysis for the e-business systems infrastructure for Network Services, I saw a couple of things. We knew that many national accounts weren't going to use our order entry system to key in orders. They would have their own system. But unless we could check off a box on a checklist that, yes, we had a web-based ordering system, we wouldn't make it past the first cut in the screening process. So the design proposed to use an application service provider to deliver that feature on a pay-as-you-go basis. The real benefits came from electronic communications between us and the members and that was where the bulk of the proposed budget was going to be spent. These communication links would make us stronger as a core group. The investment would strengthen the organization. The conceptual design met our basic needs and provided the most cost efficient way to do so. The price tag was much lower than the price of the other options that were presented."

estimate the labor expenses for each kind of person for each step in the system development lifecycle: the DEFINE step; the DESIGN step; and the BUILD step.

3. Operating costs have a number of components. Estimate labor expenses for the kinds of people that will be needed for ongoing operation and support of the new system. Estimate the line charges and usage fees for the communications network and technical architecture used by the system. Obtain yearly licensing and technical support costs from vendors of the hardware and software components used by the new system.

System Benefits

There are four types of benefits provided by a new system:

1. Direct benefits are productivity increases and cost savings due to the capacity increases brought about by a new system. Define the new functions the system provides that the company does not now have. Estimate the productivity increases and labor savings that these new features provide.

2. Incremental benefits are monetary benefits that may not be solely a result of the new system but are measurable and due in some significant degree to the capabilities of the new system. This may be an increased ability to attract and retain new customers and the extra revenue that generates. It may be the new system's ability to help the company avoid bad decisions or manage and plan for certain business expenses and the reduced costs that result.

3. Cost avoidance benefits are savings related to the increased capacity provided by the new system and the company's ability to grow the business without having to hire new staff or hire as many new staff as would otherwise be the case.

4. Intangible benefits are hard to quantify into a money amount but should be identified and listed. These benefits include such things as maintenance of a competitive advantage through better intelligence and adaptability; superior service levels that solidify customer relationships; and leveraging the abilities of talented employees and increasing their job satisfaction.

TIPS & TECHNIQUES

Sample Cost/Benefit Analysis

ITEM PRICING SYSTEM—TOTAL ESTIMATED COSTS & BENEFITS

Project Description

Build system to assist staff of account development group to more quickly create contract proposals and explore impact of different product cost and pricing structures. Monitor status of existing contracts and provide notice before cost supports expire.

Project Cost & Benefits (Dollars in Thousands)

	Qtr 1	Qtr 2	Qtr 3	Qtr 4	Qtr 5	Totals
Hardware & Software	(7.0)					(7.0)
Development Costs	(68.5)					(68.5)
Operating Costs	0.0	(1.2)	(1.2)	(1.2)	(1.2)	(4.8)
Total Costs	(75.5)	(1.2)	(1.2)	(1.2)	(1.2)	(80.3)
Direct Benefits	0.0	8.4	8.4	8.4	8.4	33.6
Incremental Benefits	0.0	30.0	30.0	30.0	30.0	120.0
Cost Avoidance Benefits	0.0	18.2	18.2	18.2	18.2	72.8
Total Benefits	0.0	56.6	56.6	56.6	56.6	226.4
Net Benefits	($75.5)	$55.4	$55.4	$55.4	$55.4	$146.1
Cumulative Benefits	($75.5)	($20.1)	$35.3	$90.7	$146.1	
Discount Rate	5%	(5% per Qtr. = 20% Annual Discount Rate)				
Net Present Value	60.6					

Detailed Schedule of Costs

Cost of Hardware & Software (Dollars in Thousands)

Item	Description	Cost
Application Server	Server to run the system—allocate 1/3 of server cost	3.0
Personal Computers	PCs for use by staff—allocate 1/3 of cost	3.0
Visual Basic language	Allocated cost of VB programming language and tools	0.5
SQL Server database	Allocated cost of SQL Server and tools	0.5
Total		**$7.0**

Cost of Development (Dollars in Thousands)

Task	Description	Cost
Define Phase	5 days at average cost of $900 per day	4.5
Design Phase	15 days at average cost of $900 per day	13.5
Build Phase—Coding	30 days at average cost of $900 per day	27.0
Build Phase—Test & Train	30 days at average cost of $650 per day	19.5
Build Phase—Roll Out	5 days at average cost of $800 per day	4.0
Total		**$68.5**

Cost of Operation (Dollars in Thousands)

Activity	Description	Cost
Qtr 1		
Qtr 2	Incremental costs of operating the system	1.2
Qtr 3	Incremental costs of operating the system	1.2
Qtr 4	Incremental costs of operating the system	1.2
Qtr 5	Incremental costs of operating the system	1.2
Total		**$4.8**

Detailed Schedule of Benefits

DIRECT BENEFITS (revenue and cost savings due to productivity improvements)

Direct Benefit 1   Save staff time on proposal creation: 10 proposals per Qtr.; 20 Hrs. per proposal; $35/Hr.

Direct Benefit 2   Do 2 additional proposals per Qtr.; 20 Hrs./proposal; $35/Hr.

Value of Productivity Improvement (Dollars in Thousands)

	Qtr 1	Qtr 2	Qtr 3	Qtr 4	Qtr 5
Save time on proposals		7.0	7.0	7.0	7.0
Do 2 additional proposals		1.4	1.4	1.4	1.4
Total Direct Benefit	$0.0	$8.4	$8.4	$8.4	$8.4

INCREMENTAL BENEFITS (benefits due in part to new system, e.g., attract new customers, make better decisions, etc.)

Incremental Benefit 1   Win more proposals due to better pricing decisions: $30,000 per Qtr. in additional profits

Incremental Benefit 2   —

Value of Incremental Benefit (Dollars in Thousands)

	Qtr 1	Qtr 2	Qtr 3	Qtr 4	Qtr 5
Win more proposals		30.0	30.0	30.0	30.0
Incremental Benefit 2		—	—	—	—
Total Incr Benefit	$0.0	$30.0	$30.0	$30.0	$30.0

COST AVOIDANCE BENEFITS (savings related to growing business without needing to add new staff or incurring other expenses)

Cost Avoidance 1   Avoid hiring more staff as business grows: half a person per year; $35/Hr.

Cost Avoidance 2   —

Value of Cost Avoidance (Dollars in Thousands)

	Qtr 1	Qtr 2	Qtr 3	Qtr 4	Qtr 5
Avoid hiring more staff		18.2	18.2	18.2	18.2
Cost Avoidance 2		—	—	—	—
Total CA Benefit	$0.0	$18.2	$18.2	$18.2	$18.2

INTANGIBLE BENEFITS (benefits that are hard to quantify in dollar amounts but that should be identified and listed)

Maintain Competitive Advantages

- Item Pricing system should be a competitive benefit for next 2 yrs.
- After that, it will simply become a necessary tool to do business

Provide Superior Service Levels

- Provide customers and prospects with timely and accurate proposals

Increase Job Satisfaction

- Release staff from tedious and time consuming pricing calculations
- Allow staff to focus on more valuable and interesting work

Chapter Summary

The work of defining supply chain opportunities will be complete when the following five deliverables are produced:

1. A clear statement of the business goal to be accomplished

2. The performance criteria required from the system. These criteria fall into four measurement categories: 1) internal efficiency; 2) customer service; 3) demand flexibility; and 4) product development. These are the conditions of success that the system must meet.

3. A conceptual design for a system to accomplish the business goal and meet the performance criteria. The system design is composed of people, process, and technology. The conceptual design is the embodiment of the strategy being used to attain the goal.

4. A definition of the project objectives that are needed to build the system. The objectives are the things that must be built to create the system outlined in the conceptual design.

5. A cost-benefit analysis that verifies that the project is worth carrying out. The senior business executive or management group who is responsible for accomplishing the business goal that the system will address must confirm that this analysis is valid.

In formulating supply chain improvement projects, it is a far better approach to successfully carry out a sequence of small steps than to attempt to make a great leap forward and risk falling short. In an approach that involves taking a sequence of smaller steps, the stakes at each step are modest and the work is more manageable so success is easier to achieve. In the approach of taking a great leap forward, the stakes are high—the work is enormous, success is harder to achieve, and the cost of failure is high.

CHAPTER 7

Developing Supply Chain Systems

After reading this chapter you will be able to

- Understand the basics of how to organize and run a project to design and build a new supply chain system

- Appreciate some useful techniques for investigating supply chain processes and documenting the findings

- See how to flesh out a conceptual system design and produce detailed system specifications

- Understand how to create accurate project plans and budgets based on the detailed system specifications

- Evaluate progress on projects and recognize problems as they emerge

After a company defines its supply chain strategy and sets the performance targets for the markets it serves, the next step is to develop the systems needed to implement the strategy. Often existing systems need to be enhanced and new systems need to be built. This chapter presents a process to follow to create the detailed system designs and to build those systems.

An organization will frequently employ the help of consultants and software vendors to do this work. However, no company can delegate the work entirely to outsiders and expect that their best interests will be served. Companies that do not stay actively involved in this work put themselves in a very vulnerable position where they "depend on the kindness of strangers..." as the character Blanche DuBois said in the play *A Streetcar Named Desire* (Williams, Tennessee, 1947, *A Streetcar Named Desire*, New York, NY: Viking Penguin).

Organizing the Systems Development Project

In Chapter 5 a three-step process to create new systems was introduced. The three steps in this process are: define; design; and build. The first step (define) is also discussed in that chapter. This chapter presents the last two steps in the process. Use this three-step process to organize the project. Each step has a certain amount of time and budget that should be allocated to it. Organize and run the project so that the work that needs to be done in each step is done within the boundaries of these time and budget limits.

There is a short list of six principles that should be used to run a project. If these six principles are consistently applied, the probability of success for the project is very high. If any one of these principles is ignored then special precautions must be taken to compensate for that. If two or more principles are violated, then the project is almost sure to fail.

1. *Every project needs a full-time leader with overall responsibility and the appropriate authority (the project leader).*

   There must be a single person who is responsible for the project's success and totally focused on getting the job done. This person must also have the authority to make decisions and act. It is good to have a steering committee or management oversight group in place that the project leader reports to, but a committee cannot make decisions in a timely manner. If there is no one person in this role, then the project progress and cost will reflect that. Progress will be slow or nonexistent and costs will be high.

2. *Define a set of measurable and nonoverlapping objectives that are necessary and sufficient to accomplish the project goal or mission.*

It is crucial that you define clear project objectives so that the people who are assigned the responsibility to achieve these objectives know what is expected of them. It is very important that the boundaries of these objectives do not overlap because if they do, the overlap will cause confusion and conflict between the teams assigned to achieve these overlapping objectives.

Make sure that each objective is absolutely necessary to the accomplishment of the project goal. Do not pursue an objective just because it seems like a good idea. Finally, you must be able to say that if each objective is achieved, then the mission or goal has been accomplished. The objectives must cover everything that needs to happen.

3. *Assign project objectives to teams of two to seven people with hands-on team leaders and the appropriate mix of business and technical skills.*

Put together a project team of two to seven people who in your judgment have among them the necessary business and technical skills and experience to address the issues that will arise in achieving the objectives you delegate to them. A team is a group of people with complementary skills who organize themselves so that all members can contribute their strengths and not be penalized for their weaknesses.

Each member of the team concentrates on the aspects of designing and building the system that they are good at and/or most interested in. For the most part, no one is required to do things they are not interested in or not good at. Within a team, the operative word is "we," not "me." The whole team is rewarded for successes and takes responsibility for mistakes. Singling out superstars or scapegoats undermines team morale and performance.

4. *Tell the teams WHAT to do but not HOW to do it.*

Point a project team in the right direction by giving them a well-defined project goal and clearly identify the project objectives that they are responsible for. The objectives define the things that they must do to be successful. The project goal and the objectives that are delegated to a team define the game that you want that team to play. The team itself must then go through the process of creating their plan to achieve the objectives that you have laid out for them.

General Patton said, "Tell people what you want but don't tell them how to do it—you will be surprised by their resourcefulness in accomplishing their tasks." The teams can make changes or additions to the objectives they are given as long as the project leader agrees that the modified objectives are still necessary and sufficient to accomplish the project goal.

5. *Break project work into tasks that are each a week or less in duration and produce something of value to the business every 30 to 90 days.*

Encourage project teams to structure their project plans so that individual tasks are a week or less in duration. Each task must have a well-defined deliverable. Track these tasks as either started, delayed, or finished. Do not fall into the trap of tracking tasks by their percentage of completion as it is unclear what "percent complete" really means. What matters is whether the task deliverable has been produced and if not, when it will be produced. The project leader must be able to track progress at the task level of detail in order to understand what is really going on and to keep accurate projections of the time to complete and the cost to complete for each of the project's objectives.

Multi-week tasks make progress hard to measure and they are the ones that will cause cost overruns and confusion. Multi-week tasks being reported by the percent complete method usually seem to be making good progress and then in the last week they suddenly turn out to be nowhere near completion and need several more weeks to complete. To avoid this problem, break big tasks into a set of sub-tasks that take a week or less to complete.

These tasks should combine to produce something that is of value to the business every 30 to 90 days. This provides the opportunity for the business to verify that the project is on the right track. It also provides deliverables that the business can start to use even before the entire project is complete and begin recouping the cost of the project.

6. *Every project needs project office staff to work with the project leader and team leaders to update plans and budgets.*

The project plan and budget are analogous to the profit and loss statements for a business. They must be updated continuously and accurately in order to provide the people running the project with the information they need to make good decisions. There is a common but misguided notion that the project leader and team leaders should be the ones who keep the plans updated. This is analogous to the idea that the president of a company and its managers should spend their time keeping the company's books. The project leader and the team leaders are responsible for creating the initial plan and budget, but after that, they must devote their full energies to making the plan a reality.

Just as there is an accounting department to keep the company's books, there needs to be a project office group that keeps the project's plans and budgets. The project office staff reports to the project leader and they work with the team leaders on a weekly basis to review and update the plans and budgets associated with each team's objectives. In this way the project leader can accurately monitor project progress and the team leaders are able to focus on running their teams and not filling out reports.

TIPS & TECHNIQUES

Organizing and Running Projects

Principles for Running Projects

1 Every project needs a full-time leader with overall responsibility and authority.

2 Define a set of measurable and nonoverlapping objectives that are necessary and sufficient to accomplish the project goal or mission.

3 Assign project objectives to teams of two to seven people with hands-on team leaders and the appropriate mix of business and technical skills.

4 Tell the teams WHAT to do but not HOW to do it.

5 Break project work into tasks that are each a week or less in duration and produce something of value to the business every 30 to 90 days.

6 Provide project office staff to work with the project leader and team leaders to update plans and budgets.

Designing Supply Chain Systems

The purpose of the design step is to flesh out the conceptual system design and create the detailed system specifications. This step also creates the detailed project plan and budget needed to build the system. This is where the people who will work on the project get to take a look at what senior management wants and figure out how they will do it. This is where adjustments and refinements are made to the project objectives as the people who have to build the system consider the realities of the job before them.

By the end of the design step it is usually possible to predict the success or failure of the project. If the people on the project finish this phase with a clear set of system design specifications and confidence in their ability to build a system to these specifications, then the project will succeed. If the opposite occurs, if the design specifications are vague, incomplete, or hard to understand and if people are ambivalent or uneasy about their chances for success, then the project will fail.

The phase begins with the project leader reviewing the project goal, the conceptual system design, and the objectives with the project work group. The work group is composed of business and technical people who have the necessary mix of business and technical skills and experience needed to do the detailed system design. It is important for the people to understand senior management's intentions and the project's goal. Specific issues relating to the project objectives and budget can be investigated during this phase. If necessary, adjustments can be made in light of the findings that come out of this phase.

Once the people on the project work group understand the goal and the objectives, they participate with the project leader to lay out a detailed plan for the work in this phase. There are two main things that need to be done in the design phase:

1. Create detailed process flow diagrams for the new system;

2. Build and test the system prototype (i.e., the user interface and the technical architecture).

Use the technique called "time boxing" to lay out a work schedule and get things done according to that schedule. Divvy up the time allotted to the total design step among the two major design activities. Break each activity into a set of tasks. Then give each task the time needed to do a competent job. Avoid the temptation to spend extra time doing excessive amounts of analysis and checking and re-checking the results that come out of each activity.

The design step should take somewhere from one to three months to complete. For the most part, work on each of these two activities can proceed simultaneously or "in parallel." In some cases the work can be done in less than one month. In no case is it wise to let the work take longer than three months. If the design work takes longer than three months, that indicates a lack of clear focus or a lack of effective organization (or both) on the project.

Supply Chain Process Mapping

The project team should review the system performance criteria as described in the define phase. The criteria will be some mix of performance targets from the four categories:

1. Customer Service

2. Internal Efficiency

3. Demand Flexibility

4. Product Development

Before starting to sketch out the detailed process flows of the new system, the project leader needs to lead people on the project teams in brainstorming exercises on ways to meet these criteria. The project leader needs to encourage a free flow of ideas and help the project group to avoid falling into the trap of premature criticism and dwelling on why things cannot be done. Focus instead on how things might be done. Generate as many ideas as possible for how to meet these performance criteria. These ideas are the raw material to be worked with and blended together to create the designs for the new system process flows.

System Prototyping to Design New Systems

Once new process flows have been designed, system prototyping is a technique to use to design a new system that will effectively support these new processes. The process decomposition diagrams provide the processing logic and sequences to be used and indicate the kinds and volumes of data that the new system needs to handle.

There are two kinds of system prototypes: user interface prototypes and technical architecture prototypes. An analogy is to think of designing a building. If you were designing a building you would create two kinds of designs. The first is the floor plan and façade of the building to show what the building will look like. The second kind is the design of the structural, electrical, and plumbing components needed to support the specified floor plan and façade. This design shows how the building will be built.

When designing systems, the user interface can be thought of as the floor plan and façade because it shows what the system will look like and how a person would move through the system. The equivalent of the structural engineering for a building is the technical architecture of a system—the hardware, operating system, and database software that will be used to support the user interface.

Both the user interface and the technical architecture designs are created in parallel. It is an iterative process that makes trade-offs between the user interface, the system functionality, and the underlying technical architecture. The aim is to find an overall design that provides a good balance between system functionality and ease of use. Look for ways to minimize the complexity of the underlying technical architecture. The key is to find ways to use relatively simple technical architectures to creatively support a wide variety of user interfaces and system features.

Prototype the User Interface for the System

Much has been written and said about the design of user interfaces for computer systems. One of the most important concepts is that the user interface should be "intuitively obvious." This means that a person who

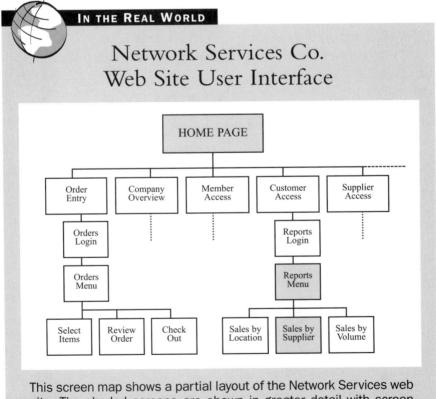

IN THE REAL WORLD

Network Services Co.
Web Site User Interface

This screen map shows a partial layout of the Network Services web site. The shaded screens are shown in greater detail with screen layouts below.

Network Services Home Page

This is the home page for the Network Services site (www.nsconline.com). Different user options are selected by clicking on the buttons shown along the left-hand side of the screen.

Reports Menu

Customers can select the report they want and set report parameters such as location, supplier, and time period.

Data Display Screen

The resulting report can be displayed either on screen or down-loaded to a spreadsheet on the customer's PC.

already knows how to do the activity that the computer system is designed to support should find that they can figure out the basics of using the new computer system in about 20 minutes of playing around with the system and trying things. The better a system interface design, the less the amount of training that is needed to teach a person to use it.

Create a prototype of the user interface based on the work done to define the process flows. The process decomposition diagrams will tell you what activities are performed in what sequence and what data are needed to support these activities. Design sequences of computer screens that map closely to the process flows and that allow the user to manipulate the data involved in these processes.

Prototype the Technical Architecture for the System

As the system user interface design is progressing, a parallel design effort is underway to select and test the technical components that will be used to build the system. Decisions should be made on the computer hardware and software to be used. The database and other packages must be specified and a programming language chosen if there is custom coding to be done. All of these components must be assembled in a test environment and tried out to see if they work as advertised. Connect the pieces and make sure they actually do work the way the vendors said they would.

Until a given technical component has been in use for at least two years, it is not wise to take any published performance statistics at face value. There will not be a wide enough base of experience with the component to provide a well-balanced assessment and it will be unclear just how the performance statistics were derived. Therefore the technical people on a design team must do their own verification that all the components will work together. This means that various performance tests are devised and run to generate benchmarking data. The technical design team needs to make changes in the component selection or even the technical architecture design if certain components prove to be incapable of performing as desired.

The database package must be installed on the hardware and operating system platform on which it is intended to run. Any packaged application software that will be used must be installed. Then test data needs to be loaded into the database and performance trials conducted to test the operation of the whole architecture. Simple code should be written to pass data from one component to the next to test out the data interfaces and the speed of LAN, WAN, and Internet connections. By the end of the prototyping activities, the technical architecture must be shown to perform up to the requirements of the new system that it will support. If a prototype cannot be created that performs well, then there is no sense in trying to build a production version of the system using this same technical architecture.

The System Design Process

The first part of the design phase should be spent in sessions where the business and technical people explore different process designs. Here is where people should "think outside of the box" and generate as many ideas as possible. The team then selects the most useful ideas and fits them together to form a coherent and detailed map of how work will be organized and how things will be done in the new business process flow.

Once the process flows have been sketched out, then the design sessions can begin to focus on how technology will be used to support this process. The design team starts to define how people in the process will interact with the technology supporting the process. Look for ways to automate the rote and repetitive work and look for ways to empower the problem solving and decision making tasks. People usually don't like to do the rote and repetitive work because it is boring but they do like doing problem solving and decision making work because it is creative and involves interaction with others.

Often the mistake is made of trying to have computers do the problem solving and decision-making work. Remember that people are the spark that animates a business process, not computers. Design systems that will be a rewarding experience for people. Design systems where people are in control and not computers. Empower people with access to information so that they can solve problems faster and make better decisions. Have computers do the rote and repetitive work. That's what computers do well.

If the decision is made to use a packaged software application, then that package should be brought in and installed in a test environment.

Realistic usage scenarios need to be scripted out. The databases used by the package need to be loaded with a sampling of real data. People who will both use and support the package then need to evaluate it by working through the usage scenarios.

Create the Detailed Project Plan

Toward the end of the design phase, as the detailed design specifications are produced, everyone involved will have a clear idea of the work they need to do and how long this will take in the build phase. The project leader is now able to oversee the creation of a detailed project plan and budget for building the system. Project teams are assigned responsibility for specific objectives and the people on these teams can then lay out the sequence of tasks they will perform to achieve each objective assigned to them. Working with project office staff, each team lays out the plan for their work. Each task has time and resource requirements assigned to it so a cost for each task can be calculated.

Respect the six principles for running projects. The project leader should let each team define how they will do their work and how long it will take. The project leader should challenge the teams to set ambitious but achievable time frames. Teams should also be encouraged to break their work into discrete tasks that take one week or less because the week is the standard unit of time in business and teams must strive to accomplish something of measurable value each week. If a certain task takes longer than a week then it is probably composed of sub-tasks. Apply the technique of process decomposition to identify these sub-tasks. A project plan that clearly lays out for every person what they are expected to accomplish every week is a valuable tool for coordinating and monitoring the work of building the system. A plan at this level of detail is also the best way to arrive at an accurate and realistic project budget for the build phase.

As the project teams are each creating their specific task plans to achieve the objectives assigned to them, the project leader is combining these plans into the overall project plan. In a process that is somewhat analogous to the manner in which a general plans a campaign, the project leader plans the sequence of activities that will lead to the successful construction and roll out of the system that the design phase has specified.

Segment the project plan by objective. Devote one section of the project plan to each objective. The project leader determines the necessary sequence for achieving the project objectives and arranges the project plan to reflect this. The project teams assigned to each objective have already created detailed plans for their work. Insert the project teams' plans into the section of the project plan related to their objectives.

Look for opportunities to run activities in parallel. The more work that can be done simultaneously, the more flexible the project will be. When activities are run in sequence, a delay in one activity causes a ripple effect that delays all the other activities queued up behind it. When activities are run in parallel, a delay in one does not delay the others. Activities need to create deliverables that come together and combine at the end to achieve the objective.

The key point here is that running in parallel allows you to finish one activity and then shift resources over to help out on another activity that is delayed. Delays are inevitable on a project. A plan that does not account for delays and provide the flexibility needed to effectively respond to them is a plan whose timetable and budget will quickly be thrown into disarray and confusion, which bring with them the probability of failure.

Create the Detailed Project Budget

Project plans and budgets are just two sides of the same coin. Plans show the time, people, and material needed to get things done and budgets show the cost of the people and material over the time frames shown in the plans. Once the project plan is in place, a detailed project budget can be derived.

Estimate the labor cost for each task shown on the plan. Add in cost of equipment such computers, software, and so on. Then add in other costs as needed for items such as travel, lodging, and entertainment. These costs all directly relate to the task sequence shown on the project plan. If the project tasks are adjusted, then the budget should also be adjusted. The total of these costs is the cost of the project.

The Decision to Proceed...or Not to Proceed

At the end of the design phase, the detailed system design and detailed project plan and budget are presented to the senior management steering committee or the executive sponsor of the project. If there are doubts about the viability of the project or if the revised budget has gotten too big, now is the time to reduce the scope of the project or cancel it altogether. At this point only 20 percent to 40 percent of the total project cost will have been incurred. The business has yet to commit the major effort on the project.

A sober assessment of the system design and its prospects for success is the order of the day. Once the project moves into the build phase, it will be very hard to make significant design changes without negative impact on the budget, the completion date, and the organization of the project. Once into the build phase, all effort must be focused on building the system as specified and responding to the day-to-day issues that arise in doing so. There cannot be continuing questions and changes in the basic design of the system without throwing the whole project into confusion.

It is all too common for companies to run the design phase as a poorly defined research project. Much time is spent in detailed analysis of what already exists but only sketchy design work is done on the specifics of what the new system will be. Debates break out on many aspects of the design of the new system but no clear answers are agreed upon. Crucial design questions are deferred to the build phase. Senior managers who conceived of the project in the define phase may still be enthusiastic about the project but the people who will actually have to build the system are starting to have doubts and disillusionment is setting in.

The design phase is the opportunity for a company to reduce the risk on a project before committing large amounts of time and money to it. The more detailed the design specifications, the better the chances for building the system on time and on budget. The broader the understanding of and support for the system among both business and technical people, the greater the likelihood that the system will be used effectively and produce the desired results.

At the end of the design phase the executive sponsor and the project leader must pause and take stock of the project. Is there an air of understanding and confidence among the people on the project? Are we good to go? Is the project ready for lift-off? The answers will be evident for those who want to hear them.

If the design phase has not produced clear design specifications, if the strategic design guidelines have been ignored, if people on the project team are not confident of their abilities, then there will be no success. The project leader can only fail in these situations no matter how heroic the use of leadership skills. There is a 75 percent failure rate on IT system development projects and this is not because we are incapable as people. It is because we make fundamental mistakes in our system designs and our plans for building them.

The Build Phase

This is the "Go For It!!!" phase. Stick to your aim and resist temptations to change direction. Keep your focus and build the momentum you need to achieve the project objectives within the time boxes called for in the project plan. Activity must be tightly focused on the completion of specific sequences of tasks. This is the step where good design and planning pay off handsomely.

In this phase the project effort really ramps up. The full complement of people is brought on to fill out the project teams. Because of this, the weekly cost or "burn rate" on the project also rises significantly in the build phase. So, unlike the previous two phases, the cost of false starts and wrong turns now adds up very quickly.

The Project Office

Once the initial project plan is in place and the project enters the build phase, the project leader and the team leaders will be fully engaged in leading the project. Neither the project leader nor the team leaders will have time to do this work on their own if they are doing a good job of leading the project. However, if the project office work is not done, the project plan and budget will quickly become out of date and will cease to be the powerful coordinating and decision-making tools that they would otherwise be. The project leader and the team leaders will then be reduced to running the project "by the seat of their pants" and that leads to trouble.

Maintaining project plans and budgets is a full-time job and needs to be recognized as such in order to be successful. The project leader is analogous to the president of a company and the project office is like the accounting department. The president does not have time to keep the company's books. There are far too many other things the president needs to do to lead the company. The accounting people keep the company books up to date so the president knows where the company stands.

Since the real world never happens exactly according to plan, the project plan must be constantly updated and adjusted to reflect reality.

The plan is the map of where the project is going and the progress made to date. If this map does not accurately reflect reality then the people on the project will lose track of where they are.

There is a pervasive tendency for people to hide bad news such as delays and cost overruns. Unless the project leader takes active steps to counter this tendency, the project will run into trouble. People need to see that they will not be penalized for reporting bad news. On the contrary, they must be shown that by reporting delays and potential cost overruns as soon as they perceive them, they can improve their chances of success.

Early reporting gives everyone more time to respond effectively. People need to understand that the project office staff are there to help them keep track of what is really going on and make timely decisions. Indeed, one of the best ways to get into trouble is to hide bad news because when the truth finally does come out, there is usually very little if any time to respond effectively to the situation.

System Test and Roll Out

The first step in rolling a system from development into production is to do a system test with all the system components in place. If competent load and volume testing was done on the system prototype during the design phase, then there will be no surprises about whether or not the system technically works and can handle the work load expected of it. The purpose of system testing will be to work through a series of test scripts that subject the system to the kind of uses it is designed for and exercise various features and logic of the system. Some embarrassing logic mistakes may well emerge during system test. This is OK. That is what system test is for—to flush out and fix these kinds of errors before the system goes into beta test.

The next step is the beta test of the system with a pilot group of business users. This pilot group of users should have been involved in some way in the design phase of the project. In this way they will already have an understanding and acceptance of the need for and benefits of the new system. Nonetheless, many minor adjustments will need to be made to the system architecture and to the user interface during the beta test. The people who operate the system architecture will need to tweak different operating parameters to get the best response time and stability from the system. The people who designed the user interface will need to sit with the pilot group of business users and listen to their ideas for improvements.

The business user who works with a system day in and day out will have a different perspective on the system's features than the people who designed and built the system. Minor inconveniences in the system's operation can become major irritants to the people who have to use the system day after day. These minor inconveniences should be fixed.

As business people in the pilot group test the system and make suggestions for adjustments, the rough edges are smoothed off. In this process, advocates for the system will emerge from among the pilot group. They will feel a personal connection to the success of the system because the system will take on a look and feel that is influenced by their suggestions. These are the people who will sell the benefits of the system to the rest of the company and who will often be the ones who train their co-workers in the use of the system.

When the system first goes into production the roll out for a big system (one that affects more than one area of the business or many people in a single area) may last a while, from six months to a year. There is not a lot of new development going on during this time, but there is a steady stream of minor enhancements and bug fixes. The project team can be slimmed down but the project leader needs to stay involved during this time to facilitate the roll out and respond quickly if some unexpected obstacle arises.

In the fall of 1999 Network Services Company reviewed and updated its strategic plan. The plan called for the company to build the first version of its "web-enabled supply chain" in 2000. These systems have been enhanced and new features added since then as market needs have evolved.

Through its strategic planning process, Network saw that the biggest benefit to be gained was from using Internet technology to electronically connect all of the different computer systems of its member companies. This would allow passing files such as purchase orders, invoices, and product masters quickly and accurately between customers, members, and manufacturers. With a system such as this, Network would be able to plug into whatever electronic trading networks were evolving in the markets it served. The system to connect Network with its members, customers, and manufacturers was named "NetLink-NSC™."

The second opportunity the company saw and acted on was to make sales history data available via its web site. Since Network is the hub of the NetLink-NSC™ system, a by-product is that Network gathers a lot of valuable information that can be used by customers, members, and manufacturers. The company decided to build a data warehouse that could be accessed through report generation screens on its web site.

Many of Network's customers already had or were building their own order entry systems and they wanted to send the company purchase orders directly from their systems using either EDI or the Internet. NetLink-NSC™ would allow Network to do that. For those customers that wanted to enter orders over the web, Network decided to lease the use of a web-based order entry package from a supply chain service provider named Tibersoft.

As Network's CIO, I was given the responsibility for building this e-business systems infrastructure. It was very important to develop the infrastructure quickly and cost effectively so I used the time-boxing guidelines suggested in the define-design-build process. A team of business and technical people was assembled and they identified the company's most pressing business issues and ideas for how technology could help. These ideas were translated into a conceptual system design (see Exhibit 6.3 in Chapter 6). Within six weeks, the define phase was complete. The conceptual design and the proposed budget to develop this infrastructure were presented to the board of directors. They gave their approval to proceed with development.

Even before the define phase was finished, work began on a design and build sequence to produce a beta test version of the data warehouse that stored sales history data. This was completed quickly and provided the business with a valuable tool as well as proof that the technical architecture was viable. It also gave everyone a clear indication that the system development effort was off to a good start and would live up to expectations.

A select group of consultants was brought in to work with company IT staff. Four project teams were created—one team to design and build each of the four components of the e-business infrastructure. Two of the project team leaders were from the Network IT staff and two were consultants. There was also a two-person project office team headed by one of Network's IT managers.

The hardware and software components chosen for the systems architecture were assembled and tested out by the teams that would use them. Data was passed between the components to make sure they could work together. Response times were tested under different data volumes to verify that the system could handle the expected amounts of data. When testing was finished, we had a solid design and there wasn't any talk of, "we'll figure this out after we get into the build phase..."

As each team finished the design phase of their work, they were well positioned to launch into their build phase. Each team had a clear set of design specifications and they had been able to test and verify that the hardware and software they were going to use would meet their expectations. Because of this it was possible for each team leader to work with the project office manager to create very accurate project plans and budgets for their work in the build phase.

The first versions of all the system components were finished within nine months and demonstrated to member companies and suppliers at the Network annual trade show. The systems were well received by Network members and some members asked if they could use these systems to support their own local business as well as to handle national account customers. So a set of enhancements to NetLink-NSC™ and the data warehouse were quickly designed and built to let members use them for their local customers. In the last three months of 2000 the project team worked with Network members to roll out version 1.0 of these systems.

At the end of 2000 Network assessed its business situation and the market conditions. It defined a set of major enhancements to add to the systems it had just rolled out. These enhancements were again designed and built within nine months and demonstrated in the fall at the annual trade show. Exhibit 7.1 shows the time boxing sequence that was used on the project.

Every Friday afternoon the team leaders and I met to discuss the project. We spent several hours and reviewed the progress and the issues that each team was encountering. The project office provided accurate and updated plans and budgets for these meetings. We could all see the most current estimate of time and cost to finish each objective. We could see if work on an objective threatened to push beyond its time box or if it was likely to overrun its budget.

IN THE REAL WORLD (CONTINUED)

EXHIBIT 7.1

Network Services E-Business System Development Sequence

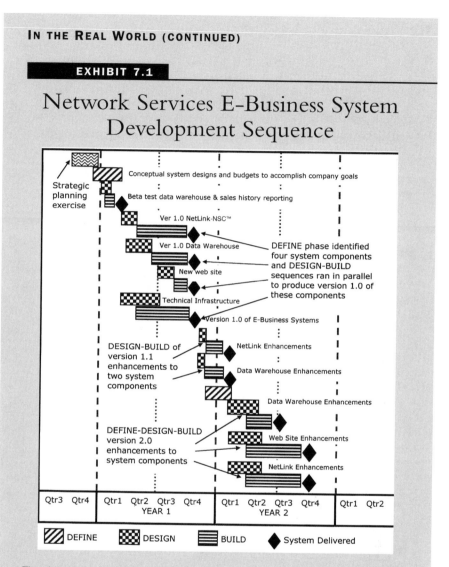

The development sequence was focused and tightly time-boxed. Work ran in parallel during the design and build phases requiring good planning and coordination. Version 1.0 of e-business systems infrastructure was created in nine months. Based on positive reception and feedback from version 1.0, enhancements for version 1.1 were created. Further assessment of business needs led to definition of next round of major enhancements that created version 2.0 of the e-business infrastructure.

IN THE REAL WORLD (CONTINUED)

In the build phase especially, the project teams were at their highest staffing levels so the project "burn rate" was also at its highest level. Small delays and little misunderstandings or scope changes could quickly balloon into big problems and cost overruns. Having regular weekly review sessions backed up by current and accurate project plans showed me early on where problems were developing. This way I knew when and where I needed to get personally involved to keep things moving.

Chapter Summary

Design Step Deliverables

1. A detailed design for the business process flow of the system. Also, agreement among the people who will have to work with the system that it will meet the performance criteria expected of it.

2. A system prototype that specifies both the technical architecture and the user interface. This technical architecture must be shown to be capable of handling the data volumes and user demands that are expected. There must be a complete set of screen layouts, report formats, and specifications for all aspects of the user interface.

3. There must be a detailed project plan and budget that accurately reflects the time, cost, and resources needed to build the system.

Build Step Deliverables

1. A working system that matches the design specifications and meets performance criteria. The building of the system should be scheduled so that there is something of value delivered to the business every 30 to 90 days. This means that certain pieces of the system must be finished and put into use before the entire system is completed.

2. A complete and updated set of technical design documents. The design documentation is analogous to the wiring diagrams and structural plans of a building.

3. A complete set of operating instructions. The people who operate and maintain a system are different from the people who build systems. The people who operate a system need to know how to bring the system up, bring it down, do performance tuning, and do troubleshooting and operating maintenance.

CHAPTER 8

The Promise of the Real-Time Supply Chain

After reading this chapter you will be able to

- Appreciate the "always-on" connection and what it means

- Assess the profit potential inherent in the self-adjusting feedback loop

- Explore how the power of the self-adjusting feedback loop can be harnessed to drive your supply chain

- Discuss the concept of emergent systems

The pace of business change and innovation is both exciting and relentless. Over the next decade innovative companies in different market segments will learn to design and deploy their supply chains to improve their competitive position in the markets they serve. They will create supply chains that enable them to develop and deliver products and provide levels of service at price points that their competitors cannot match.

We all sense that something profound has happened in the last ten years or so. The Internet is a part of it, but it is not only about the Internet. We learned that in the "dot com" bubble of the late 1990s and early 2000s. There is something more than just the Internet going on here.

The Start of Something Big

As a historical analogy, consider what happened some 200 years ago at the beginning of an age that came to be known as the Industrial Age. The people of the time sensed that a powerful potential had been released by the invention and spread of the steam engine.

The steam engine for the first time provided a movable source of power that could be generated on demand and efficiently harnessed to perform a wide variety of tasks. The Industrial Age was not so much about the steam engine as it was about the things that could be done and were done with the power that the steam engine made available. Once it was born, the Industrial Age went on to outgrow the steam engine as it evolved more advanced engine technologies such as internal combustion, the jet, the electric motor, and atomic power.

The rise and spread of the Internet has created for the first time a global, multi-directional communications network that is "always-on." The cost of connecting to this network is so cheap that there is no need for companies to save money by staying off line and only connecting periodically. The normal state for companies is transitioning from being off line and unconnected to one of being on line and connected.

As more and more companies use the Internet and other communications networks to create always-on connections with each other, they will find ways to share data that enable them to better coordinate their interactions. They will also learn faster and adapt to changing conditions faster. These capabilities will clearly result in efficiencies that can be turned into business profits.

The always-on connection is a new light that sheds steady illumination on a landscape that had before been seen only in periodic snapshots. We are experiencing something similar to seeing a sequence of still photos turn into a moving picture. As more pictures are taken at shorter intervals, you cease to see a sequence of still photos and instead come to see a continuous, moving image. This continuous, moving image is what we see as we move from the snapshot or batch-time world into the real-time world.

Supply chain management is a process of coordination between companies. Those companies that learn to coordinate in real-time will become incrementally more and more efficient. They will become more profitable and quicker to see new opportunities than their competitors who are still working in a batch-time world of snapshot pictures.

The Profit Potential of the Self-Adjusting Feedback Loop

The self-adjusting feedback loop is a very useful phenomena. An example is the cruise control in an automobile. The cruise control constantly reads the vehicle's actual speed and compares that to the speed it was set for. It responds to bring the actual speed in line with the desired speed. It causes the engine to either accelerate or decelerate. The cruise control's goal is to achieve and maintain the desired speed. As the vehicle travels down the highway it continuously monitors speed and operates the engine to achieve its goal.

Other examples of a self-adjusting feedback loop at work are a thermostat that controls the temperature in a room, or a guided missile that zeros in on a heat source or a radar emission source. Self-adjusting feedback loops use negative feedback to continuously correct their behavior. Negative feedback occurs when a system compares its current state with its desired state (or goal) and takes corrective action to move it in a direction that will minimize the difference between the two states. A continuous stream of negative feedback guides a system through a changing environment toward its goal.

Companies can learn to work together to achieve supply chain performance targets that are profitable to all of them. They can learn to constantly adjust their behavior day after day, hour by hour to respond to events and continue to steer toward their performance targets. The bullwhip effect can be controlled by the introduction of negative feedback to dampen down the wild demand swings that otherwise result.

The opportunity now exists to leverage the power of the self-adjusting feedback loop across entire supply chains. Real-time data sharing and close coordination between companies can be employed to deliver operating efficiencies that result in significant profits over time. The result of these continuous incremental adjustments to supply chain operations is analogous to the growth of capital over time due to the miracle of compound interest.

Harnessing the Feedback Loop to the Supply Chain

How can the power of the self-adjusting feedback loop be brought to bear in a supply chain? The answer is beginning to appear. As companies link up using always-on communication networks to conduct business with each other, they begin to automatically collect useful data as a by-product of their interactions: electronic purchase orders, order status, order receipts, invoices, and payment status. It is no longer a huge administrative chore to regularly track performance in the areas of customer service, internal efficiency, demand flexibility, and product development.

Customers are starting to use supply chain "report cards" to grade the performance of their suppliers. The report cards are more accurate and more frequently produced than was previously possible. The next step is for companies to move beyond the use of these report cards as merely convenient tools for beating up their suppliers. The opportunity exists for customers and suppliers to use this data to work together to meet mutually beneficial performance targets. Companies can select performance targets that will generate quantifiable benefits and profits to reward them for the effort needed to achieve the targets.

Either one dominant company can set the performance targets or groups of companies can negotiate among themselves to set targets. The important thing is that all participating companies in a supply chain believe the targets are achievable and that when they are achieved there will be rewards as a result. The desire to receive these rewards is what brings the self-adjusting feedback loop into being.

The feedback loop happens when peoples' interactions with each other are cast in the form of a game whose object is to achieve the performance targets. If companies and people in a supply chain have real-time access to the data they need then they will steer toward their targets. If they are rewarded when they achieve their targets then they will learn to hit these targets more often than not. The profit potential of negative feedback and the self-adjusting supply chain is now unleashed.

Playing the Game of Supply Chain Management

Human beings are social creatures who love to play games. This is a good thing because through playing games we constantly learn and improve our skills and our performance. Companies such as Wal-Mart and Dell and their supply chain partners have in many ways begun to create an evolving game out of managing their supply chains. They have steadily learned and developed supply chains that are better than those of their competitors and that are clearly business advantages for them.

There are only a few things required to start a game. In his book, *The Great Game of Business*, Jack Stack lays out the four conditions that are needed (Stack, Jack, 1992, *The Great Game of Business*, New York, NY: Currency/Doubleday). They are:

1. People must understand the rules of the game and how it is played. They must know what is fair and what is not fair and how to score points.

2. People must be able to pick the roles or positions they want to play in the game. They also need to get the training and experience necessary to keep developing the skills they need to succeed in their positions.

3. All players must know what the score is at all times. They need to know if they are winning or losing and they need to see the results of their actions.

4. All players must have a personal stake in the outcome of the game. There must be some important reward, either monetary or psychological, that provides a reason for each player to strive to succeed.

Basically, the game of supply chain management is a relatively simple game, as is soccer or basketball. Which is not to say that any of these games can be mastered without years of practice and play. The main techniques and operations of supply chain management are well enough understood to be taught to a wide range of people in different supply chain positions (see Chapters 2 and 3). The Internet is the way for everyone to know the score at all times and see the results of their actions. Profits generated by operating efficiencies provide people with rewards and the reason to strive to succeed.

In supply chain management, everyone can acquire and install technology so technology alone cannot constitute a significant competitive advantage. The advantage lies in the way the game is played. Let's go back to the example of Alexander the Great (see Chapter 1). His army did not have any technology that was not also possessed by his opponents. In fact Alexander deliberately used less technology. He simplified his army's operations and equipment in order to make it more mobile and more efficient. His army could travel faster and lighter than those of his adversaries.

Advantage goes to those players who learn to use simple technology and simple tactics extremely well. Alexander's soldiers were well trained in how to use their technology and because of the simplicity of their tactics, they could remember and use them effectively in the heat of the moment when it really counted. After all is said and done, success is often just a matter of consistent performance and making fewer errors than your competition.

EXECUTIVE INSIGHT

Emergent behavior is what happens when an interconnected system of relatively simple elements begins to self-organize to form a more intelligent and more adaptive higher-level system. Steven Johnson in his book, *Emergence—The Connected Lives of Ants, Brains, Cities, and Software*, explores the conditions that bring about this phenomenon.

In an interview with Steven Johnson I posed six questions and asked him to share his insights on a number of topics. These topics range from what gives a system emergent characteristics to how companies could organize their supply chains so as to encourage and benefit from emergent behavior.

1 What is an "emergent system?" How is an emergent system different from an assembly line?

"The catchphrase that I sometimes use is that an emergent system is 'smarter' than the sum of its parts. They tend to be systems made up of many interacting agents, each of which is following relatively simple rules governing its encounters with other agents. Somehow, out of all these local interactions, a higher-level, global intelligence 'emerges.' The extraordinary thing about these systems is that there's no master planner or executive branch—the overall group creates the intelligence and adaptability; it's not something passed down from the leadership. An ant colony is a great example of this: colonies manage to pull off extraordinary feats of resource management and engineering and task allocation, all by following remarkably simple rules of interaction, using a simple chemical language to communicate. There's a queen ant in the colony, but she's only called that because she's the chief reproductive engine for the colony. She doesn't have any actual command authority. The ordinary ants just do the thinking collectively, without a leader.

"A key difference between an emergent system and an assembly line lies in the fluidity of the emergent system: randomness is a key component of the way an ant colony will explore a given environment —take the random element out, and the colony gets much less interesting, much less capable of stumbling across new ideas. Assembly lines are all about setting fixed patterns and eliminating randomness; emergence is all about stumbling across new patterns that work better than the old ones."

❷ You say that such systems are "bottom-up systems, not top-down." These systems solve problems by drawing on masses of simple elements instead of relying on a single, intelligent "executive branch." What does this mean for people who are trying to design and build emergent systems?

"One of the central lessons, I think, is that emergent systems are always slightly out of control. Their unpredictability is part of their charm, and their power, but it can be threatening to engineers and planners who have been trained to eliminate unpredictability at every turn. Some of the systems that I've looked at combine emergent properties and evolutionary ones: the emergent system generates lots of new configurations and ideas, and then there's a kind of natural selection that weeds out the bad ideas and encourages the good ones. That's largely what a designer of emergent systems should think about doing: it's closer to growing a garden than it is to building a factory."

 What does it mean when you say that emergent systems display complex adaptive behavior?

"The complexity refers to the number of interacting parts, like the thousands of ants in a colony, or the pedestrians on a street in a busy city. Adaptive behavior is what happens when all those component parts create useful higher-level structures or patterns of behavior with their group interactions, when they create something, usually unwittingly, that benefits the members of the group. When an ant colony determines the shortest route to a new source of food and quickly assembles a line of ants to transport the food back to the nest; when thousands of urbanites create a neighborhood with a distinct personality that helps organize and give shape to an otherwise overwhelming city, these are examples of adaptive behavior."

 What is negative feedback as opposed to positive feedback? What role does negative feedback play in the ability of a system to exhibit adaptive behavior?

"Negative feedback is crucial, and it's not at all negative in a value-judgment sense. Positive feedback is what we generally mean when we talk about feedback, as in the guitar effect that we first started to hear as music in the 60s: music is played through a speaker, which is picked up by a microphone, which then broadcasts it out though the speaker, creating a sound that the microphone picks up, and so on until you get a howling noise that sounds nothing like the original music. So positive feedback is a kind of self-perpetuating, additive effect: plug output A into input B which is plugged into input A. Negative feedback is what you use when you need to dampen down a chain like this, when there's a danger of a kind of runaway effect, or when you're trying to home in on a specific target. Think of a thermostat trying to reach a preset temperature: it samples the air, and if the air's too cold, it turns the heat on, then samples it again. Without negative feedback, the room would just keep getting hotter, but the thermostat has been designed to turn the heat off when the air reaches the target temperature. Ants use a comparable technique to achieve the right balance of task allocation throughout the colony: an individual ant who happens to be on foraging duty will sample the number of ants also on foraging duty that she stumbles across over the course of an hour. If she encounters a certain number, she'll switch over to another task (nest building, say) in order to keep the colony from becoming overrun with foragers."

❺ In your book you mention a designer who has proposed building a learning network of traffic lights that will find an optimal solution to continually changing traffic conditions. You observe that, "You can conquer gridlock by making the grid itself smart." What is it that would make the grid smart? Is this grid an example of an emergent system?

"The idea proposed in the traffic model is not to take the traditional engineering, top-down approach and say: 'Let's look at the entire city and figure out where all the problems are, and try to design the roads and the light system to eliminate the problems.' The smart grid approach is to give each light a local perspective with a little bit of information, and give it the goal of minimizing delays at its own little corner. So the light would be able to register the number of cars stacked up at the intersection, and it would be able to experiment with different rhythms of red and green, with some feedback from its near neighbors. When it stumbles across a pattern that reduces delays, it sticks to that pattern; if the delays start piling up again, it starts experimenting again. The problem with this sort of approach is that on Day One it's a terrible, terrible system, because it doesn't yet know anything about traffic flows. (You'd have to teach it quite a bit before you could actually implement it.) But it would learn very quickly, and most importantly, it would be capable of responding to changing conditions in a way that the traditionally engineered approach would not. That's a hallmark of adaptability."

 Consider a system composed of many different companies whose goal is to provide a market with the highest levels of responsiveness at the lowest cost to themselves. High levels of responsiveness require that these companies work together to design, make, and deliver the right products at the right price at the right time in the right amounts. What are some of the things that these companies could do to organize themselves into an emergent system?

"There's a telltale term in supply chain systems, which may well be unavoidable—the term 'chain' itself. Almost all emergent systems are networks or grids; they tend to be flatter and more horizontal, with interaction possible between all the various agents. The problem that supply chains have with positive feedback revolves around the distance between the consumer and those suppliers further down the chain; because the information has to pass through so many intermediaries, you get distortion in the message. Most emergent systems that I've looked at have a great diversity of potential routes that information can follow; the more chain-like they become, they less adaptive they are. The other key here is experimentation: letting the system evolve new patterns of interaction on its own, since these can often be more useful and efficient than the preplanned ones. Of course, you don't want to waste a few economic quarters experimenting with different supply chains, most of which are a disaster. But that's where some of the wonderful new modeling systems for complex behavior can be very handy: you can do the experimenting on the computer, and then pick the best solutions to implement in real life."

Emergent Behavior in Supply Chains

In the workings of a system such as a free market we witness emergent behavior. This behavior is what the great British economist Adam Smith referred to as the "invisible hand" of the market. This invisible hand emerges to set product prices so as to best allocate available supplies to meet market demands. Local interactions between large numbers of agents, governed by simple rules of mutual feedback, produce a macro effect for the system as a whole that results in what we call emergent behavior.

As we begin to practice supply chain management as a game between companies and people who are motivated to achieve certain performance targets, we will see emergent behavior in supply chains. Good players in the supply chains of particular markets will seek each other out because by playing together they can create more efficient supply chains and generate better profits.

Supply chains will form up like sports teams and these teams will compete with each other for market share. Just as the game of basketball or soccer evolves over time, so too will the game of supply chain management. New tactics, techniques, and technology will come about. Market demands and the desire for competitive advantage will drive companies to collaborate and innovate with each other to win at the game of supply chain management.

Computers are best used to automate the rote, repetitious activities that humans find to be dull and boring. These are all the ongoing and routine activities of recording and monitoring supply chain operations. Computers do these tasks very well. They do not fall asleep, they do not miss details, and they can handle enormous volumes of data without complaint.

People are best used to do the creative and problem solving activities. These are the activities that do not have clear right or wrong answers.

These are the activities that call for people to collaborate with other people and share information and try out different approaches to see which ones work best. People are good at these activities and they like doing them so they learn and keep getting better.

At a macro level, this will give rise to supply chains that, in effect, learn and grow smarter. Computers will listen to the hum and crackle of data flowing through the real-time, always-on supply chain. They will employ pattern recognition algorithms to spot exceptions and events that need to be brought to the attention of human beings. Like good pilots and navigators, people will learn to respond effectively to these developments as they happen. People will learn to keep steering the supply chain on a course toward its desired performance targets.

Adaptive Networks and Economic Cycles

As we learn to recognize and effectively respond to developments in our supply chains it will tend to lengthen the periods of market growth and stability. Any industry or market where there is a boom to bust cycle is an opportunity for us to apply the self-adjusting feedback loop to smooth out the economic ups and downs. The boom to bust cycle is caused by the same dynamic that results in the bullwhip effect in individual supply chains.

In industries ranging from electronics manufacturing to real estate development to telecommunications, the boom to bust cycle causes economic waste and disruption. It also brings with it all the related human hardships that are caused by the cycle. The ability to recognize and smooth out excessive swings in demand, prices, and productive capacity in different areas of the economy will create greater stability. And through this stability more wealth will be both generated and preserved. Think of the wealth that was destroyed by the excessive investments that created more dot com companies and more telecommunications capacity than were needed. Think of the wealth that disappeared in the company closures and job losses that happened when these companies and their suppliers finally had to face the consequences of too much supply and not enough demand.

Adaptive supply chain networks using real-time information and negative feedback can effectively dampen excessive market swings. This ability alone will have a wealth creation effect that is even more powerful than what was created by the effect of the steam engine.

Chapter Summary

The "always-on" connection of the Internet and other communications networks allows us to see ourselves in real-time. We can now see the supply chain as a continuous moving picture whereas in the past we could only see it as a collection of snapshots taken at periodic intervals. This always-on, moving picture makes it possible to constantly adjust supply chain operations week to week and day to day to get significant new efficiencies.

This self-adjusting feedback loop is harnessed to the supply chain through the daily actions of the people who carry out supply chain operations. First motivate people by providing them with monetary or psychological rewards for achieving predefined performance targets. Then provide people with real-time information that shows them whether they are moving toward or away from their targets. People will steer toward their targets and they will learn to hit these targets more often than not.

The effect of this dynamic will be to give rise to supply chains that are both highly responsive and very efficient. Real-time operating adjustments will result in supply chains that can better adapt to business changes and deliver performance and profitability that is of a higher level than anything that has been seen before.

Additional Resources

1. Books

Chopra, Sunil, and Peter Meindl, 2001, *Supply Chain Management: Strategy, Planning, and Operations*, Upper Saddle River, NJ: Prentice-Hall, Inc.

Fredendall, Lawrence D., and Ed Hill, 2001, *Basics of Supply Chain Management*, Boca Raton, FL: St. Lucie Press.

Goldratt, Eliyahu M., 1984, *The Goal*, Great Barrington, MA: The North River Press Publishing Corporation.

Graham, Gordon, 1987, *Distribution Inventory Management*, Richardson, TX: Inventory Management Press.

Johnson, Steven, 2001, *Emergence: The Connected Lives of Ants, Brains, Cities, and Software,* New York, NY: Scribner.

Roman, Eugene R., 1996, *Reengineering the Distributor*, South Holland, IL: Systems Design, Inc.

Senge, Peter M., 1990, *The Fifth Discipline: The Art and Practice of the Learning Organization*, New York, NY: Doubleday/Currency.

Stack, Jack, 1992, *The Great Game of Business*, New York, NY: Currency/Doubleday.

2. Magazines & Journals

EBN, Manhasset, NY: CMP Media, Inc.

Journal of Business Logistics, Oak Brook, IL: Council of Logistics Management.

Supply Chain Technology News, Cleveland, OH: Penton Media, Inc.

3. Internet

Council of Logistics Management, *www.clm1.org*

Integrated Business Communications Alliance, *www.ibcaweb.org*

Stanford Global Supply Chain Forum, *www.stanford.edu/group/scforum*

Supply-Chain Council Home Page, *supply-chain.nidhog.com*

Supply Chain Management Research Center,
www.cio.com/research/scm

Uniform Code Council, *www.uc-council.org*

4. Professional Organizations

The Council of Logistics Management

2805 Butterfield Road, Suite 200, Oak Brook, IL 60523,
Ph: (630) 574-0985

The Supply-Chain Council

1150 Freeport Rd., Pittsburgh, PA 15238,
Ph: (412) 781-4101

This list of additional resources just barely scratches the surface. The reader should also use Internet search engines such as Google (*www.google.com*) and do a further search. Another useful search resource are online book sellers such as Amazon (*www.amazon.com*) and Barnes & Noble (*www.bn.com*).

Index

7-Eleven, 31

A

activity cycle time, 148,149
adaptive behavior, 243
adaptive networks, 247–248
advanced planning and scheduling systems, 127–128
Aero Exchange International, 135
aggregate planning, 54–55
Alexander the Great, 7–9, 240–241
Alexy, James, 169–171
always-on connection, 236–238, 248

B

beer game, 104–105
big box store format, 18–19
Breed Technologies, 101
broadband, 122–123
build to order (BTO), 144–146, 149
build to stock (BTS), 144–145, 149
bullwhip effect, 104–106, 114–115, 118–119, 238, 247
  demand forecasting, 107
  order batching, 108
  performance incentives, 110
  product pricing, 109
  product rationing, 109
burn rate, 225
Burton, Donald, 95–97
business cycle, 103–104
business strategy, 30
  aligning the supply chain, 31–37
  business opportunities, 177
  strategy creation, 178–182
  See also core competencies
  See also conceptual system design

C

cash-to-cash cycle time, 147
Chopra, Sunil, 2, 9, 32, 38–40, 50, 126, 249
collaborative planning, forecasting, and replenishment (CPFR), 115–117
  how to start, 118–119
competitive advantage, *see* business strategy
complex adaptive behavior, 243
conceptual system design, 181, 183–191
core competencies, 20–23, 33–40, 99–101
cost benefit analysis (CBA), 199–205
Covisint, 135
credit and collections, 70–73
crossdocking, 11–12, 94
customer relationship management (CRM), 129
customer service, 65–66,80, 130–131, 141, 180
  customer service metrics, 144–146, 149
cycle inventory, 12, 59, 63

D

data sharing, 164–171
data warehouse, 158–163
days sales outstanding (DSO), 71
DC. *See* distribution center
debt to net worth, 152
delivery scheduling, 91, 95–97
  delivery sources, 93
  direct deliveries, 91
  generalized assignment, 92–93
  milk run deliveries, 92
  savings matrix technique, 92–93
Dell Computers, 38–40, 117, 239
demand flexibility, 142, 148–150, 163, 178
demand forecasting, 48–50
  forecasting methods, 50–53
  forecasting variables, 49–50